ISBN: 9781290930550

Published by:
HardPress Publishing
8345 NW 66TH ST #2561
MIAMI FL 33166-2626

Email: info@hardpress.net
Web: http://www.hardpress.net

W. WORDSWORTH.

MEMOIRS

OF

WILLIAM WORDSWORTH,

COMPILED FROM AUTHENTIC SOURCES;

WITH

NUMEROUS QUOTATIONS FROM HIS POEMS,
ILLUSTRATIVE OF HIS LIFE AND CHARACTER.

BY JANUARY SEARLE,

AUTHOR OF "LIFE, CHARACTER, AND GENIUS OF EBENEZER ELLIOTT,"
"LEAVES FROM SHERWOOD FOREST," ETC.

LONDON:
PARTRIDGE & OAKEY, PATERNOSTER ROW.

MDCCCLII.

INTRODUCTORY REMARKS.

William Wordsworth is the father of a new school of Poetry, and his name marks an era in the literature of England, which is full of deep interest to the philosophical inquirer. He began his career with profound convictions respecting the nature and functions of poetry; its dignity as an art, and the immense capabilities it afforded for the utterance of sublime and ennobling truths, and for the furtherance of human liberty and happiness. He saw, too, that the old Harp of the Bards was profaned by the touch of uninspired, and even frivolous hands; and he determined, if possible, to rescue it from their keeping, and restore it once again to its divine uses, and ancient melody. To accomplish this grand object, he devoted all his faculties and culture, and was so deeply impressed with the idea that this was his especial mission upon earth, that he retired amongst the mountains and lakes of Westmoreland—a solemn and lonely man—holding converse with the Invisible through the Visible forms of Nature, and thus fitting himself for the priestly office to which he aspired. And in all the years of his noviciate—through all the time when, by universal acclamation, he stood crowned with the sacred laurels of the Bard—and his mission was accredited by all men—he never for a moment flagged in his purpose, or stooped to the garlands of fame,—but gathering his prophet's mantle around him, he pursued his undeviating course, alike regardless of applause, condemnation, and persecution. He had looked well into his own heart, before he set out on his perilous enterprise; had measured well his own strength of purpose, and capability of performance; knew, in short, what he had to do, and did it.

To appreciate fully, however, the historical position of William Wordsworth, and the value of his labours, it will be necessary to take a retrospective view of the literature which preceded him, or at least to state its leading characteristics. The grand old era of Shakspeare and his cotemporaries had long since passed away, and the noble music of Milton's song had ceased to thrill the hearts and souls of men. The brilliant, half-inspired writers in the reign of Queen Anne, who came to represent the national mind at the close of our Augustan epoch, had formed a school of Poetry in England,—at once witty and sententious, profound and hollow; without heart or genius; and with nothing but talent and culture to recommend it. Pope, who may be considered the head of this school, set the seal of his intellect upon the cotemporary and subsequent literature of that era. He had rivals whom he stung to silence, and covered with contempt by his satires, and imitators whom he fondled and despised. Pope and his compeers were, however, kings and priests of song, compared with the herd of twangsters who succeeded them. The fancy and wit, the philosophy and refinement of Pope, were sunk and lost in the barrel-grinding of these imitators of his style; and Poetry was stripped of its subjective attributes, and lived only as a mechanical form.—This at all events is true of the writers professedly of the Pope school; and the few exceptions, for upwards of fifty years after his death, owe what little fame they possess to their own little originality.

In all the departments of literature, the same lifelessness and uniformity were manifest. The deadest materialism prevailed both in science and philosophy, and the national soul seemed paralyzed beneath the weight of a dire, unknown, unseen incubus of death. In the meanwhile, however, there were influences at work both in England and Europe, which were silently preparing the way for a revolution in the thoughts and opinions of men. The spiritual element awoke in Germany and France, and like a mighty, but half-blind god, began to react upon the materialism of the age. Then, for the first time since the close of the Commonwealth, did the pulse of England begin, also, to beat with the music of life and health. The importations of German sentimentality—mawkish and imbecile as they often were—touched the right chords in the English heart, and roused it to consciousness.

Men saw that there was new life struggling under this ghastly utterance, and began to lose their faith in the dead formalism, which they had so long hugged in their idolatry. Their minds were gradually turned to the old grandees of Elizabeth's reign: to Shakspeare and rare Ben Jonson, and to Spenser, Beaumont and Fletcher, until, at last, the reactionary currents had fairly set in, which were to cleanse the national mind of its disease, and restore it to health. Add to this, that the higher minds of England were already immersed in those metaphysical speculations which, whilst they confirmed the increasing spiritual tendency, gave earnestness to their aim and character. And when, at last, after Rouseau and Voltaire —the two poles of the great revolutionary idea of Europe—had flung their works into the cauldron of this vast, seething, reactionary fermentation—the wonderous phenomenon, which we call the French Revolution, burst upon the world—the reaction was complete, and a new epoch dawned upon man—the epoch, viz., of progress and humanity—which will never close until its mission is sealed with the liberty and happiness of mankind.

Such, then, is a slight sketch of the characteristics of the age into which Wordsworth was born. He came in time to catch the full surges of its influence, and his spirit was one of the few destined to aid the onward tide of events, and mould their flowing forms into a fixed and plastic beauty. Not, however, by any active mingling with the affairs of men, for this was clearly no part of his vocation, but by silent watching and contemplative thought, and the faithful exercise of his poetic faculties. The political arena was open to more daring, and less costly men, who could do their temporary work and disappear without farther loss to the nation : but the poet had a greater and more enduring work to accomplish ; he was to become the architect of a new literature and the singer of a new gospel of life to the world. The growing earnestness of his age demanded a voice to speak for it—many voices, indeed, each in its proper province of feeling and of thought. And in no province was this voice more loudly called for than in that of poetry, for death reigned in all the courts of the poetic temple, and every priest was a corpse which the muse had stuck about with flowers, that she might conceal even from herself the sorrowful fact of her desertion and utter misery.* Wordsworth came to tear away the mask, and spurn the dead from her temple.

The great object of Wordsworth's life was to win men back, by his poetic example, to an admiration and love of the natural in all its aspects. To him nature is not only divine and glorious as a whole, but equally so in all her parts. In the meanest worm that crawls, in the tinyest flower and the rankest weed; in the summer foliage, and in the brown skeleton leaves of autumn; in the lonely mountain, and the silent stream—he recognizes the spirit of beauty, and she passes through *his* spirit into song, and becomes at once a poem, and a grand moral gospel. All things in heaven and earth are consecrated existences to him, no matter how profanely and lowly they may rank with common observers.

And this view of Nature he carries into the presence of man. It is not kings and the

---

*These remarks do not of course apply to Cowper and Burns, to whom our modern literature is so deeply indebted, but to their predecessors, from Pope downwards.

mighty ones in the dream-play of Life whom he thinks to be the only worthy subjects for poetry. If these people come in his way, he is Catholic enough to admit them through his imagination, into the immortality which awaits his books. But he does not *seek* them. He thinks they have already had their full share of poetic honour, and perhaps more than their due share; that so much dwelling upon such people, with their unrealities and false glares of splendour, has diseased the holy faculty of the poet, and turned his visions into morbid night-mares. It seems in short to be his opinion, that the higher we advance in the social scale, the further we are off from the sanities and truths of human life. He consequently looks for these in ruder and humbler ranks: in the dwellings of the poor, in the hearts of the peasantry, and the intuitions of uncorrupted childhood. He delights to sing of the commonest things, and is ever happy in his delineations of the hopes and fears, the loves, inquietudes, and disappointments of rustic existence. He has the minute anatomical power of Crabbe, combined with a still higher physiological and creative faculty, by which he not only lays bare the hidden meaning and laws of natural objects, but transforms the objects themselves into new beauty and significance. The grey light of morning breaking over the hill tops of his chosen retreat—the hot sunshine burning in white molten silver upon the bosom of his enchanted lakes—the lonely fisherman upon their shores—look truer and more affecting objects, as we gaze upon them, through the medium of his musical sorcery of words. His picture of the poor wandering leech gatherer, over the deep black pools of the wild moor, with the profound moral which he has attached to it, is an instance of his skill as a painter, and of his divine insight as a man of genius. "The Idiot Boy," is another specimen of his consummate ability to render the most inert and painful nature alive and glorious by the spiritual appliances of his art. This boy, detached from the poet's mind, is a gloomy and sorrowful spectacle; but when *he* enters the shattered temple in which the Idiot dwells, and unites him, by the magic of his presence, to the great universal temple of Nature, he is no longer a gloomy insanity, but a poetically created existence. We see that this Idiot also has a soul; a subject soul certainly, and bound to what we might call hard conditions of capability and action, but a soul nevertheless: vital with its own vagarious life, and rejoicing in it. Wordsworth's revelations of the inner workings of this Idiot's mind—of the dark moon glimmerings which break impulsively through the ruins of his intellect, and make him wild with joy or ghastly with terror —are unsurpassable achievements.

And yet Wordsworth is abused for his tameness and want of inspiration! Dead asses and idiots, Peter Bells and Waggoners, it is said, are not elevated facts enough for poetry! The foolish objectors do not understand how all poetry is based upon facts, and how the most obscure things become purified and poetic, when they are raised by imagination, and placed in new connections of thought. It is the province of the Poet to elevate the homely, and to beautify the mean. To him, indeed, nothing is mean, nothing worthless. What God has made, he, the exponent of God, shall love and honour.

It is our acknowledged want of sympathy with the common, which induced Wordsworth to devote his life and attention to the awakening of it. He knew that whatever is touched by genius is converted into gold, and stamped thenceforth as sacred, by the impress of its image. The Betty Foys of human existence, although they, too, are " encompassed by eternity," and destined to the same futurity as the Queens Elizabeth and Mary, have never, before Wordsworth's time, had a poetic priest high enough to make them religious by his love and fidelity to them. It required immense faith and majesty of mind to hazard the experiment; so plebeian are all Betsies that wear red cloaks and black bonnets, instead of ermines and crowns. Wordsworth, however, did not care for names and orders, but saw and worshipped humanity alone. He has dared, therefore, to say and to maintain, through a long and honourable life, that Elizabeth Foy was as much of a man as Elizabeth Queen. He has linked together the throne and the cottage through all their manifold gradations. He has, of course, had his full share of abuse for this heroic and triumphant effort; but the good old Skiddaw-granite-rock of a man was not to be moved by abuse, but continued to sing and preach in his solitude, with the solemnity and witchery of a Memnon statue.

It should be remembered, also, that Wordsworth purposely avoids the florid style in the architecture of his verse. His ideal model is the plain severity of the Saxon temple, in which the grand and the simple were united.—He *aims* at clear and unmistakeable utterance. His chaste simplicity is the work of *an artist*, and by no means the necessity of a limited intellect. If this fact were borne in mind by his detractors, it is not unlikely that they would be less furious when they speak of him. For an author should always be read, measured, and judged by his own standard, and not by ours.—Nothing can be more absurd than the subjection of a poet to any critical canon or authority. Knowing his position as an expounder of the hidden truths of the universe—as an oracle of the Infinite, and a revealer of the beauty and mystery of nature and human life—he stands in our presence like the Hebrew *law-giver*, covered with the golden glory and lightning of the Highest, whom he has *seen* upon the summits of Sinai. Henceforth we are to accept his law, not he ours.

It is useless to question and criticise in our foolish manner the new bard of God, whoever he may be, or under what circumstances soever he may appear among us. *He* does not live by questionings and logical inductions, but by faith and inspiration. Entranced in the miracle of his own existence, with all these vast orbs of immensity pressing upon his brain, and the silent creatures of the fair earth stealing like noiseless musical shadows into the temple of his soul, he has no time to consult the critics whether this or that mode of reproducing them is the orthodox one. He will speak in any way he can; and if the old grey-beard world *will* be startled or shocked at his speech, he has no other answer for it but this: "My utterance is the birth-cry of my thoughts."

Every new poet—every genius indeed that is divine—is a notification to us that the world of things is about to be classified anew, and to assume a deeper meaning. And certainly one would think that so great an announcement might gladden the hearts of men, instead of making them savage and ferocious at it. For of all men the poet is highest and noblest. He is the awful Seer, who unveils the spirit of Nature and looks with solemn and unscathed eyes upon her naked loveliness and terror.

The Beloved of God, he is admitted into the very presence of the Invisible, and reports, in such wild and strange words as he can find, the sights he has beheld there. He is the renovator of man and Nature. He lifts the human soul upon his daring wings, and carries it into light and immortality. In his words we behold the re-creation of the universe. We see Orion, like the starry skeleton of a mighty giant, go forth into the solitudes of unfathomable space; we witness the planting of the solar stars, and hear the everlasting roar of the vast sun, as it wheels, seething from God's hands, upon its fiery axis; and these unspeakable sights are heightened in their magnificence and terrific grandeur by the poet, who holds us fast to their symbolical meaning, and chains them to the being of God, as the expressions in appearance of His thoughts and will.

By virtue, therefore, of his mission, the poet is Antinomian. He is master of all law, and no critic can trammel him. Let him try that, and the poet, like the war-horse who snuffs the far-off battle, will say to the little man—" Ha! ha !"

It is necessary that we here make a few extracts from Wordsworth's defence, if we may call it so, of his manner of writing, in order that the reader may be prepared for a right appreciation of his poetry. In speaking of his poems as a whole, he says:—

"The principal object proposed was to choose incidents and situations from common life, and to relate or describe them, throughout, as far as was possible, in a selection of language really used by men, and, at the same time, to throw over them a certain colouring of imagination, whereby ordinary things should be presented to the mind in an unusual aspect; and further, and above all, to make these incidents and situations interesting, by tracing in them, truly though not ostentatiously, the primary laws of our nature; chiefly as far as regards the manner in which we associate ideas in a state of excitement. Humble and rustic life was generally chosen, because, in that condition, the essential passions of the heart find a better soil in which they can attain their maturity, are less under restraint, and speak in plainer and more emphatic language; because in that condition of life our elementary feelings coexist in a state of greater simplicity, and, consequently, may be more accurately contemplated and more forcibly communicated; because the manners of rural life germinate from these feelings, and from the necessary character of rural occupations, are more easily comprehended and are more durable; and lastly, because in that condition, the passions of men are incorporated with the beautiful and permanent forms of Nature. The language, too, of these men has been adopted (purified indeed from what appear to be its real defects, from all lasting and rational causes of dislike or disgust), because such men hourly communicate with the best objects from which the best part of language is *originally* derived; and, because, from their rank in society, and the sameness and narrow circle of their intercourse, being less under the influence of social vanity, they convey their feelings and notions in simple and unelaborated expression. Accordingly, such a language, arising out of repeated experience and regular feelings, is a more permanent, and a far more philosophical language, than that which is frequently substituted for it by poets, who think that they are conferring honour upon themselves and their art in proportion as they separate themselves from the sympathies of men, and indulge in arbitrary and capricious habits of expression, in order to furnish food for fickle tastes, and fickle appetites, of their own creation."

It will be seen from this extract, that Wordsworth has no sympathy with the inflammations of Literature. His mission is with the ordinary, the beauty and philosophy of which he has devoted his life to expound. He has flung a charm over existences which Nature did not seem before him to love as her children; and we honour him for the great work which he has accomplished.

MEMOIR OF
WILLIAM WORDSWORTH.

WILLIAM WORDSWORTH was born at Cockermouth, in Cumberland, on the 7th of April, 1770. His father, John Wordsworth, was an attorney, and law-agent to Sir James Lowther, who was afterwards raised to the peerage, and created Earl of Lonsdale. His mother's name was Anne Cookson, only daughter of William Cookson, a mercer of Penrith, and of " Dorothy, born at Crackenthorpe, of the ancient family of that name, who, from the time of Edward the Third, had lived in Newbiggen Hall, Westmorland." *His grandfather was the first of

*Memoirs of William Wordsworth, by Dr. Wordsworth, vol. 1, page 7.

the name of Wordsworth who came into Westmorland, where he purchased the small estate of Stockbridge. His ancestors had lived at Peniston, in Yorkshire, probably before the time of the Norman Conquest. "Their names," says Wordsworth, in his *Autobiographic Memoranda*, " appear on different occasions in all the transactions, personal and public, connected with that parish; and I possess, through the kindness of Colonel Beaumont, an almery made in 1525, at the expense of a William Wordsworth, as is expressed in a Latin inscription carved upon it, which carries the pedigree of the family back four generations from himself."

The poet was second son of his father, and spent most of his early days at Cockermouth. He was subsequently removed to Hawkshead grammar school. And here, properly speaking, his true history begins. In the "Prelude," a poem but lately published, we have a full account of his boyish ways, and experiences, and a complete record of the development of his mind.

This poem is, therefore, doubly valuable, both as a psychological and literary performance.

True it is that, like all Wordsworth's poems, on their first appearance, it has been exceedingly well abused, and that too by men who have eyes to see, and understandings wherewith to understand; which is singular; but the poem is not the less a great vestibule, or outer porch to a great poetic temple for all that. In reading it, I seem to be walking up through the long dim avenues of eternity with the young soul of the poet, and listening to its half remembered ideas of the unspeakable glory from which it has come—itself radiant with immortal lustres—and bursting out, ever and anon, in an ecstacy of rapturous wonder at the mystic and beautiful revelations of Time—the grand and everflowing pageantry of nature,—its woods, mountains, streams, and heavenly hosts of stars. For it is certain that this, or something like this, is the impression one receives, whilst following the poet, in the manifold disclosures which he makes of his own spiritual and mental development: he will not let go the glory of his birth, but cleaves to it, as to the title of some grand heritage, which he shall one day possess. And it is this, and its kindred spiritual ideas, which give the mystic tinge and colouring to all Wordsworth's higher poetry, as if it had been baptised in an element altogether alien to sensuous experience, and to the common world of man.

It was a long time, however, before Wordsworth could understand Nature,—before he could make out what she would be at, in dodging him in his ordinary paths, and haunting him in his solitary hours. True, he was always very fond of the beautiful and terrible Mother; loved her storm-wrath, and wind-wrath; her golden and voluptuous sunshine; her rivers and brooklets; her mountains, lakes, dells, and the flowery bespanglement of her green and rustling kirtle. But this was all. He did not know that this love was merely initial,—the basework of a deeper passion—the basement of a divine wisdom. And although he was always a wayward and lonely boy, yet he *was* a boy, and his roots did not strike up precociously, and burst him into a man at once; but took time to grow; so that the boy was father to the man. Neither would Nature allow him to brood too intently over her wonders and loveliness, but took him gently captive, in a sort of side-winds, or brief revelations of herself, in his rambles and hunting sports; for he was made of too good stuff to be spoilt by any over-doings —and she was jealous of her favourite.

It was very fortunate for Wordsworth that his early life was cast in the midst of such magnificent scenery, as that of Cumberland, for it acted powerfully upon his mind, and helped to mould his character, and develope his genius. School did very little for him, nor College, nor even books, until a comparatively late period of his life. But both nature and poetry had always a great and transcendent charm for him. As a boy, at Cockermouth he obtained the rudiments of learning from the Rev. W. Gillbanks; and his father, who was a man of vigorous character, and considerable culture and scholarship, initiated him into the pantheon of poetry, by repeating to him the finest passages of Shakspeare, Milton, and Spenser, which the boy subsequently committed to memory. But he was frequently refractory in his conduct, and peevish in his temper. His mother, whom he loved much, and who died before he was eight years of age, had at times terrible misgivings about her darling son, on these accounts, although I find no record to justify her in her forebodings. He was certainly a wild little fellow, full of animal spirits, which never flagged, with a little of the dare-devil in him: but this is natural enough in a healthy boy. Wordsworth, in alluding to his mother's dread of the "evil chance" of his life, gives us an anecdote, with the intention of justifying her, which seems to me very comical in such connection.

"I remember going once," he says, "into the attics of my grandfather's house at Penrith, upon some indignity having been put upon me, with an intention of destroying myself with one of the foils which I knew was kept there. I took the foil in my hand, but my heart failed me.

"Upon another occasion, while I was at the same house, along with my eldest brother, Richard, we were whipping tops together in the large drawing-room, on which the carpet was only laid down upon particular occasions.— The walls were humg round with family pictures, and I said to my elder brother: 'Dare you strike your whip through that old lady's petticoat?' 'No,' he replied, 'I won't.' 'Then,' said I, 'here goes!'—and I struck my lash through her hooped petticoat; for which, no doubt, I was properly punished, although I have forgotten it. But, possibly from some want of judgment in punishments inflicted, I was perverse and obstinate in defying chastisement, and rather proud of it than otherwise."

Perhaps the real truth of Mrs. Wordsworth's anxiety is, after all, to be found in the fact that she had anticipated an extraordinary career for her son. There does not appear, however, to have been much ground for the supposition that the "evil chance" would prevail; and considering the wise teaching of this dear mother, and the apt though erratic nature of her son, I think there was good reason for a more cheering augury of his fate. Speaking of his mother's mode of education, in the "Prelude," he says, that it was founded upon

> "a virtual faith, that He
> Who fills the mother's breast with innocent milk,
> Doth also for our nobler part provide,
> Under His great correction and control,
> As innocent instincts, and as innocent food.
> . . . .
> This was her creed, and therefore she was pure
> From anxious fear of error, or mishap,

And evil, overweeningly so called,
Was not puffed up by false, unnatural hopes,
Nor selfish, with unnecessary care;
Nor with impatience for the season asked
More than its timely produce; rather loved
The hours for what they are, than from regard
Glanced on their promises in restless pride.
Such was she—not for faculties more strong
Than others have, but from the times, perhaps,
And spot in which she lived, and thro' a grace
Of modest meekness, simple-mindedness,
A heart that found benignity and hope,
Being itself benign."

That there are evidences of this healthful and pious faith, this holy and beneficent teaching, in Wordsworth's writings, every one acquainted with them will admit; and the passage just quoted is more than ordinarily interesting on this account, as an illustration of the force of early training. His mother's love haunts him in later years, although he is altogether silent about his father, and only speaks of his mother twice in all his poems. The hearth-stone, and its gods, seem to have been too sacred with him for parade. When he appears before the vicar, with a trembling, earnest company of boys about his own age, to say the catechism, at Easter, as the custom was, the mother watches him with beating heart; and here is the second tribute of affection to her beloved memory:

> "How fluttered then thy anxious heart for me,
> Beloved mother! Thou whose happy hand
> Had bound the flowers I wore, with faithful tie;
> Sweet flowers, at whose inaudible command,
> Her countenance, phantom like, doth reappear;
> Oh! lost too early for the frequent tear,
> And ill-requited by this heart-felt sigh."

With such a mother as this, it is no wonder that Wordsworth—in spite of his occasional devilry—was a happy and joyous boy. He looks back, indeed, in after life, upon the home and scenes of his childhood, as upon some enchanted region. He has no withering recollections of poverty or distress; all is sunshine and delight. The sweet, melodious, and romantic Derwent is the syren of these dreams, and it sings with wondrous music in his verse. All his memories are associated with the fine scenery of his birth-place—are fused into it—and become, at last the real foundation of his life: and here is a description of his native scenery, which I find ready made to my hand:

"The whole district may be said to stand single in the world, and to have in the peculiar character of its beauty no parallel elsewhere. It is in the concentration of every variety of loveliness into a compass which in extent does not greatly tax the powers of the pedestrian, that it fairly defies rivalry, and affords the richest pabulum to the poetical faculty. There, every form of mountain, rock, lake, stream, wood, and plain, from the conformation of the country, is crowded with the most prodigal abundance into a few square miles. Coleridge characterises it as a 'cabinet of beauties.' 'Each thing,' says he, 'is beautiful in itself; and the very passage from one lake, mountain, or valley to another, is itself a beautiful thing again.' Wordsworth, in his own 'Description of the Country of the Lakes,' dwells with the zest and minuteness of idolatry upon every feature of that treasury of landscape. The idea he gives of the locality is very perfect and graphic. If the tourist were seated on a cloud midway between Great Gavel and Scafell, and only a few yards above their highest elevation, he would look down to the westward on no fewer than nine different valleys, diverging away from that point, like spokes from the nave of a wheel, towards the vast rim formed by the sands of the Irish Sea. These vales —Langdale, Coniston, Duddon, Eskdale, Wastdale, Ennerdale, Buttermere, Borrowdale, and Keswick—are of every variety of character; some with, and some without lakes; some richly fertile, and some awfully desolate. Shifting from the cloud, if the tourist were to fly a few miles eastward, to the ridge of old Helvellyn, he would find the wheel completed by the vales of Wytheburn, Ulswater, Haweswater, Grasmere, Rydal, and Ambleside, which bring the eye round again to Winandermere, in the vale of Langdale, from which it set out. From the sea or plain country all round the circumference of this fairy-land, along the gradually-swelling uplands, to the mighty mountains that group themselves in the centre, the infinite varieties of view may be imagined —varieties made still more luxuriant by the different position of each valley towards the rising or setting sun. Thus a spectator in the vale of Winandermere will in summer see its golden orb going down over the mountains, while the spectator in Keswick will at the same moment mark it diffusing its glories over the low grounds. In this delicious land, dyed in a splendour of ever-shifting colours, the old customs and manners of England still lingered in the youth of Wordsworth, and took a firm hold of his heart, modifying all his habits and opinions. Though a deluge of strangers had begun to set in towards this retreat, and even the spirit of the factory threatened to invade it, still the dalesmen were impressed with that character of steadiness, repose, and rustic dignity, which has always possessed irresistible charms for the poet. Their cottages, which, from the numerous irregular additions made to them, seemed rather to have grown than to have been built, were covered over with lichens and mosses, and blended insensibly into the landscape, as if they were not human creations, but constituent parts of its own loveliness. In this old English Eden, all his schoolboy days, Wordsworth wandered restlessly, drawn hither and thither by his irresistible passion for nature, and receiving into his soul those remarkable photographs which were afterwards to delight his countrymen. There can be no doubt that the charms of this lake scenery added still more strength to the poet's peculiar tendencies, and developed a conservative sentiment, which, though temporarily overcome, afterwards reared itself up in haughtier majesty than before. The poet was naturally led to indulge much in out-of-door wanderings and pastimes, such as skating, of which he has left a picture unapproachable in its vividness and precision."

In such scenery then, and with such occupations, did the boy spend his time, until it became necessary to send him to a higher school than Cockermouth afforded. He was accordingly dispatched to Hawkshead Grammar School, near the lake of Esthwaite, where he was not crammed with overmuch learning. He speaks of these larger school days with enthusiasm, in his "Prelude;"—not, however, because the little Latin and mathematics which he learned were so tasteful to his mind; but because his leisure hours and holidays were rendered sweeter by the restraints of the school, and gave a greater zest to his field-sports, and the secular books which he loved. He mentions his amusements—such as birds' nesting, in the warm moist mornings of Spring,—springing woodcocks, in the brown and mellow days of

Autumn, — bathing in the Derwent, that "tempting playmate" of his, into which, even when five years old, he would plunge again and again, " making one long bathing of a Summer's day,"— rowing, on sunny half-holidays with his boisterous schoolmates, on the great " plain of Windermere,"—or skating, by day and night, upon the frozen bosom of Esthwaite. His beloved books, too, at this time, find a record in his verse. They are Fielding—that mighty creator, so full of the "*play-impulse*," like an old god who makes worlds, and amuses himself with the story of their various fortunes; Cervantes, who laughed Christendom out of its chivalry, because chivalry was dead as an institution, and had become laughable; Le Sage, with his Shaksperian knowledge of life, and his inimitable artistic power; and Swift, with his sharp wit, learning, and satire, glittering amid continents of mud. " Gulliver's Travels," and the " Tale of a Tub," were the things which stuck to him fastest, however, of all the works of these writers.

In the meanwhile the poet was awakening within him, and the poetic pabulum was becoming, every day, more and more necessary to his existence. His fine receptive spirit stored up all the forms and influences of nature; revivified them, and reproduced them by its power. The strong individuality, which marks his poetry, manifested itself at this early period; for he loved solitude better than his playmates; although he loved them too, and speaks of them with affection; but the dells, mountains, and lakes, were his most beloved companions.— Often would he lie down upon the grass or the heather, and wait for the gentle voices which had so frequently whispered the secrets of nature in his ears, and by their inspiration had enabled him to catch a glimpse of the divine glory behind the veil of things; or looking upwards into the blue unfathomable depths of heaven, he has asked questions which those depths could not answer, and has thus tasted of the sorrow which makes life holy. His own mind had begun to react upon Nature, and to make her more beautiful or terrible, according to his mood. He began to feel the *auxiliar light*, which comes from the soul, and diffuses its glory over all things, making the common noble, and investing the grandest forms of the material world, with the still grander attributes of imagination. He hints at the process of all this; at the "plastic power" and the creative power,—the outer and the inner modus of his culture. "A plastic power," he says—

> " Abode with me; a forming hand, at times
> Rebellious, acting in a devious mood;
> A local spirit of his own, at war
> With general tendency; but for the most
> Subservient strictly to external things
> With which it communed. An auxiliar light
> Came from my mind, which on the setting sun
> Bestowed new splendour; the melodious birds,
> The fluttering breezes, fountains that run on
> Murmuring so sweetly in themselves, obeyed
> A like dominion; and the midnight storm
> Grew darker in the presence of my eye."

And all this was much better than school-learning—although school learning is not to be despised. But Wordsworth, as before remarked, learned very little at school, although he took honours in the great Alma Mater, out of doors. And it is singular that nearly every one who has made a figure, and left a mark in the world's page, has been equally unindebted to school for his success. Genius hates to be put in harness, and yet without discipline of some sort or other, there can be no stability of character—no steady aim, purpose, or achievement. Nature always takes care to exaggerate the natural tendency of her favourites, that the balance may be restored by discipline, and that the work which she requires of the peculiar faculties may be done. And to this discipline genius itself must, in the end, submit, or fail in the high purpose of its existence. We can afford that it should be a little erratic, and wild in its ways, especially in youth; that it should even like the song of the birds better than the concords of grammar. But it must learn grammar after all, and many other things beside, if it is really to do any great work in the world. And this was the case with Wordsworth, who alternated his book studies with those of Nature. For although he acquired nothing more than the mechanical forms of learning at Hawkshead—and these were limited to Latin and mathematics—yet the discipline was good for his health, and the acquirements themselves were not to be despised. In the meanwhile, he had written verses too remarkable to be passed over without notice, although the poet himself says, " they are but a tame imitation of Pope's versification, and a little in his style." They were written upon the completion of the second centenary of the foundation of the Hawkshead grammar school (in 1585, by Archbishop Sandys,) as a school exercise, when Wordsworth was only fourteen years old ; and as the poetry is not included in his works, although Dr. Wordsworth has preserved it in the autobiographical memoranda of his " Memoir," lately published, I will make a quotation from it, that the reader may see how the genius of Wordsworth first adapted itself to the laws and formulary of poetic art. It is *Education* that speaks in the following lines.

> " There have I lov'd to skim the tender age,
> The golden precepts of the classic page ;
> To lead the mind to those Elysian plains
> Where, thron'd in gold, immortal Science reigns ;
> Fair to the view is sacred Truth display'd,
> In all the majesty of light arrayed,
> To teach, on rapid wings, the curious soul,
> To roam from earth to heaven, from pole to pole ;
> From thence to search the mystic cause of things,
> And follow Nature to her secret springs ;
> Nor less to guide the fluctuating youth,
> Firm in the sacred paths of moral truth.

To regulate the mind's disordered frame,
And quench the passions kindling into flame;
The glimmering fires of virtue to enlarge,
And purge from vice's dross my tender charge.
Oft have I said, the paths of fame pursue,
And all that virtue dictates, dare to do.
Go to the world—peruse the book of man,
And learn from thence thy own defects to scan;
Severely honest, break no plighted trust—
But coldly rest not here—be more than just!
Join to the rigour of the sires of Rome
The gentler manners of the private dome;
When virtue weeps in agony of woe,
Teach from the heart the tender tears to flow;
If Pleasure's soothing song thy soul entice,
Or all the gaudy pomp of splendid vice,
Arise superior to the syren's power,
The wretch, the chort-liv'd vision of an hour.
Soon fades her cheek, her blushing beauties fly,
As fades the chequer'd bow that paints the sky."

Now, it must be acknowledged, that this writing, imitative as it is, is very remarkable as the production of a boy of fourteen; and that it displays an uncommon degree of artistic skill in its construction, with much command of language, and a moral culture one does not often meet with in boys. This, however, was not Wordsworth's first attempt at composition.

D

" It may be, perhaps, as well to mention," says the poet, in his brief autobiographical notes, appended to the Memoir, " that the first verses I wrote, were a task imposed by my master; the subject ' The Summer Vacation ;' and of *my own accord* I added others upon ' Return to School.' These exercises, however," he continues, " put it into my head to compose verses from the impulse of my own mind; and I wrote, while yet a schoolboy, a long poem running upon my own adventures, and the scenery of the country in which I was brought up. The only part of that poem which has been preserved is the conclusion of it, which stands at the beginning of my collected poems. It commences ' Dear native regions.' " This poem was the archetype of the " Prelude," and was a good preparatory discipline to the structure of that nobly musical poem.

In 1786, in anticipation of leaving school, he wrote some sweet verses, in which he speaks, with a sad fondness, of the old region round about Hawkshead, and vows, with a lover's heart, never to forget its beauty, but to turn towards it wherever he may be, as to the shrine of his idolatry.

"Thus from the precincts of the west
The sun, while sinking down to rest,
Though his departing radiance fail
To illuminate the hollow vale,
A lingering lustre fondly throws
On the dear mountain-tops where first he rose."

The muse had now fairly possessed him, and he was destined to have a triumphant career as the high priest of song. Among his earliest sonnets is the following, which is the last quotation I shall give from these boyish effusions.

"Calm is all nature as a resting wheel:
The kine are couched upon the dewy grass;
The horse alone, seen dimly as I pass,
Is cropping audibly his later meal:
Dark is the ground; a slumber seems to steal
O'er vale and mountain and the starless sky.
Now in this blank of things a harmony,
Home-felt and home-created, comes to heal
That grief for which the senses will supply
Fresh food, for only then while memory
Is hushed am I at rest. My friends! restrain
Those busy cares that would allay my pain;
Oh, leave me to myself, nor let me feel
The officious touch that makes me droop again!"

His school-days at Hawkshead were now

drawing to a close, but before we leave this part of his life, this genial seed-time from which he subsequently reaped so glorious a harvest, it will be well to add a few more particulars respecting the locality of Hawkshead, and the general discipline of its old Elizabethan grammar school, as a sort of supplement to the previous history. And, first of all, a word about Esthwaite.

* " Esthwaite, though a lovely scene in its summer garniture of woods, has no features of permanent grandeur to rely on. A wet or gloomy day, even in summer, reduces it to little more than a wildish pond, surrounded by miniature hills ; and the sole circumstances which restore the sense of a romantic region, and an Alpine character, are the knowledge (but not the sense) of endless sylvan scenery, stretching for twenty miles to the sea-side, and the towering groups of Langdale and Grasmere fells, which look over the little pasture barrier of Esthwaite, from distances of eight, ten, and fourteen miles.

" Esthwaite, therefore, being no object for

*De Quincy, Tait's Magazine, for 1839.

itself, and the sublime head of Coniston being accessible by a road which evades Hawkshead, few tourists ever trouble the repose of this little village town. . . . . Wordsworth, therefore, enjoyed this labyrinth of valleys in a perfection that no one can have experienced since the opening of the present century. The whole was one paradise of virgin beauty; and even the rare works of man, all over the land, were hoar with the grey tints of an antique picturesque; nothing was new, nothing was raw and uncicatrized. Hawkshead, in particular, though tamely seated in itself and its immediate purlieus, has a most fortunate and central locality, as regards the best (at least the most interesting) scene for a pedestrian rambler. The gorgeous scenery of Borrowdale, the austere sublimities of Wastdalehead, of Langdalehead, or Mardale,—these are too oppressive in their colossal proportions, and their utter solitudes, for encouraging a perfectly human interest. Now, taking Hawkshead as a centre, with a radius of about eight miles, we might describe a little circular tract which embosoms a perfect net-work of little valleys—separate wards or cells, as it were, of one large valley, walled in by the great primary mountains of the region. Grasmere, Easdale, Little Langdale, Tilberthwaite, Yewdale, Elterwater, Loughrigg Tarn, Skelwith, and many other little quiet nooks, lie within a single division of this labyrinthine district. All these are within one summer afternoon's ramble. And amongst these, for the years of his boyhood, lay the daily excursions of Wordsworth.

"I do not conceive that Wordsworth could have been an amiable boy; he was austere and unsocial, I have reason to think, in his habits; not generous; and above all, not self-denying. . . . . Meantime, we are not to suppose that Wordsworth, the boy, expressly sought for solitary scenes of nature amongst woods and mountains, with a direct conscious anticipation of imaginative pleasure, or loving them with a pure, disinterested love, on their own separate account. These are feelings beyond boyish nature, or, at all events, beyond boyish nature trained amidst the necessities of social intercourse. Wordsworth, like his companions, haunted the hills and the vales for the sake of angling, snaring birds, swimming, and sometimes of hunting, according to the Westmorland fashion, on foot: for riding to the chace is often quite impossible, from the precipitous nature of the ground. It was in the course of these pursuits, by an indirect effect growing gradually upon him, that Wordsworth became a passionate lover of Nature, at the time when the growth of his intellectual faculties made it possible that he should combine those thoughtful passions with the experience of the eye and ear."

De Quincey then continues to relate, as an illustration of the sudden, silent manner in which Nature makes herself felt by the observer, even when he is paying no attention to her operations, but is occupied with nearer and more secondary matters—how he and Wordsworth were walking one midnight, during the Peninsular war, from Grasmere to Dunmail Raise, to meet the mail, in order that they might obtain the newspaper Coleridge was in the habit of sending them, and thus learn the earliest intelligence of the state of affairs on the Continent. "At intervals, Wordsworth had stretched himself at length on the high road, applying his ear to the ground, so as to catch any sound of wheels that might be going along at a distance. Once, when he was slowly rising from this effort, his eye caught a bright star that was glittering between the brow of Seat Sandal and the mighty Helvellyn. He gazed upon it for a minute or so; and then, upon turning away to descend into Grasmere, he made the following explanation:—' I have remarked, from my earliest days, that if, under any circumstances, the attention is perfectly braced up to a steady act of observation, or of steady expectation, then, if this intense condition of vigilance should suddenly relax, at that moment any beautiful, any impressive visual object, or collection of objects, falling upon the eye, is carried to the heart with a power not known under other circumstances. Just now my ear was placed upon the stretch, in order to catch any sound of wheels that might come down upon the lake of Wythburn, from the Keswick road; at the very instant when I raised my head from the ground, in final abandonment of hope for this night, at the very instant when the organs of attention were all at once relaxing from their tension, the bright star hanging in the air above those outlines of massy blackness fell suddenly upon my eye, and penetrated my capacity of apprehension, with a pathos and a sense of the Infinite, that would not have arrested me under other circumstances.'"

And it was precisely in this manner, according to De Quincy, and indeed according to the known laws by which Nature educates the faculties of the poet, that Wordsworth was educated in his boyhood. All this hunting, fishing, and rambling, were but the means by which Nature allured him to the woods and waters, that she might silently impress him with her manifold forms and influences. There are evidences, however, of something like *communion* with Nature in the early poems of Wordsworth, even before he left Hawkshead; and his solitary wanderings, his roamings round the lake of Esthwaite—five miles before breakfast—were not without a purpose, and could not have been undertaken unless an unquenchable, though perhaps not a fully developed love, had possessed his heart, for natural scenery, and the mystic lore which it teaches. His own confession, that though Nature was at first a dumb perplexing riddle to him, and merely affected him by her beauty and grandeur,—I say his own confession, that in spite of this, he subsequently felt the coming of the "*auxiliar light*" from his own soul, which penetrated her forms, and made them instinct with sublime intelligence—will illustrate the idea with sufficient force and clearness.

Enough, however, has been said upon this subject, for it is impossible to trace in any direct manner, the subtle and delicate influences of Nature upon the human mind, or to determine even, in the instance of Wordsworth, the precise time when he first sought " the woods and mountains, with a direct conscious anticipation of imaginative pleasure." We will leave all this, therefore, and direct the reader to the " Prelude," as the best exposition of the poet's mental development at this early period. A few words respecting the government of the Hawkshead grammar school, as an influence affecting the character of the poet, and we will then follow him to Cambridge.

"Taking into consideration the peculiar tastes of the person," says De Quincy, "and the peculiar advantages of the place, I conceive that no pupil of a public school can ever have passed a more luxurious boyhood than Wordsworth. The school discipline was not, I believe, very strict; the mode of living out of school very much resembled that of Eton for Oppidans,—less elegant perhaps, and less costly in its provisions for accommodation, but not less comfortable; and in that part of the arrangement which was chiefly Etonian, even more so; for in both places the boys, instead of being gathered into one fold, and at night into one or two huge dormitories, were distributed amongst motherly old " dames," technically so called at Eton, but not at Hawkshead." In the latter place, agreeably to the inferior scale of the whole establishment, the houses were smaller and more college like, consequently more like private households; and the old lady of the *menage* was more constantly amongst them, providing with maternal tenderness, and with a professional pride, for the comfort of her young flock, and protecting the weak from oppression. The humble cares to which those poor matrons dedicated themselves, may be collected from several allusions scattered through the poems of Wordsworth; that entitled " Nutting" for instance, in which his early Spinosistic feeling is introduced of a mysterious power diffused through the solitudes of woods, a presence that was disturbed by the intrusion of careless and noisy outrage, and which is brought into a strong relief by the previous homely picture of the old housewife equipping her young charge with beggar's weeds in order to prepare him for a struggle with thorns and brambles. Indeed not only the moderate rank of the boys, and the peculiar kind of relation assumed by these matrons, equally suggested this humble class of motherly attentions, but the whole spirit of the place and neighbourhood was favourable to an old English homeliness of domestic and personal economy."

It will thus be seen that Wordsworth was early inducted into those thriftful and economical habits which marked his character through life, and enabled him during his young days to bear the temporary loss of his paternal fortune without much inconvenience. And the above facts are worthy to be remembered, not only as illustrating much for us in the history of Wordsworth, but as another instance of the power of a wise and early training.

The poet thus alludes to the cottages of the "Danes:"—

> " Ye lowly cottages wherein we dwelt
> A ministration of your own was yours;
> Can I forget you, being, as you were,
> So beautiful among the pleasant fields
> In which ye stood? or can I here forget
> The plain and seemly countenance, with which
> Ye dealt out your plain comforts? Yet had ye
> Delights and exultations of your own.
> Eager, and never weary, we pursued
> Our home-amusements, by the warm peat-fire,
> At evening; when, with pencil and smooth slate,
> In square divisions parcelled out, and all
> With crosses and with cyphers scribbled o'er,
> We schemed and puzzled, head opposed to head,
> In strife too humble to be named in verse;
> Or round the naked table, snow white deal,
> Cherry or maple, sate in close array,
> And to the combat, loo or whist,* led on
> A thick-ribbed army; not, as in the world,
> Neglected, or ungratefully thrown by,
> Even for the very service they had wrought,
> But husbanded thro' many a long campaign.

* It is related by De Quincy, that during Wordsworth's early residence in the lake country—after his return from Cambridge—his mind was so oppressed by the gloomy aspect of his fortunes, that evening card-playing was resorted to, to divert him from actual despondency.

Uncouth assemblage was it, where no fear
Had changed their functions; some plebeian cards
Which fate, beyond the promise of their birth,
Had dignified, and called to represent
The persons of departed potentates.
Oh, with what echos on the board they fell!
Ironic diamonds,—clubs, hearts, diamonds, spades,—
A congregation piteously akin!
Cheap matter offered they for boyish wit,
Those sooty knaves, precipitated down,
With scoffs and taunts, like Vulcan out of heaven:
The paramount ace, a moon in her eclipse,
Queens gleaming thro' their splendour's last decay,
And monarchs surly at the wrongs sustained
By royal-visages. Meanwhile, abroad
Incessant rain was falling, or the frost
Raged bitterly, with keen and silent work;
And, interrupting oft that eager game,
From under Esthwaits' splitting scenes of ice
The pent up air, struggling to free itself,
Gave out, to meadow grounds and hills, a loud
Protracted yelling; like the noise of wolves,
Howling, in troops, along the Bothnic main."

And, then, as a specimen of the out-door sports, and exercises of his youth, whilst dwelling with his good old dame, he says:

" And in the frosty season, when the sun
Was set, and visible for many a mile

The cottage windows blazed thro' twilight gloom,
I heeded not their summons: happy time
It was, indeed, for all of us—for me,
It was a time of rapture! Clear and loud,
The village clock struck six—I wheeled about,
Proud and exulting, like an untired horse,
That cares not for his home. All shod with steel
We hissed along the polished ice in games
Confederate, imitative of the chase,
And woodland pleasures—the resounding horn,
The pack loud chiming, and the hunted hare.
So thro' the darkness and the cold we flew,
And not a voice was idle; with the din
Smitten, the precipices rang aloud;
The leafless trees, and every icy crag,
Tinkled like iron; while far distant hills
Into the tumult sent an awful sound
Of melancholy not unnoticed, while the stars
Eastward were sparkling clear, and in the west
The orange sky of evening died away.
Not seldom from the uproar I retired
Into a silent bay, or sportively
Glanced sideway, leaving the tumultuous throng
To cut across the reflex of a star,
That fled, and flying still before me, gleamed
Upon the glassy plain; and oftentimes,
When we had given our bodies to the wind,
And all the shadowy banks on either side
Came sweeping through the darkness, spinning still
The rapid line of motion, then at once
Have I, reclining back upon my heels

> Stopped short; yet still the solitary cliffs
> Wheeled by me, even as if the earth had rolled,
> With visible motion, her diurnal round!
> Behind me did they stretch in solemn train,
> Feebler and feebler, and I stood and watched,
> Till all was tranquil as a dreamless sleep."

And with this famous skating passage—the finest realization of the kind in poetry, I will conclude this outline of the poet's school-days and mental history.

CAMBRIDGE.

It was in October, 1787, that Wordsworth was sent to St. John's College, Cambridge, by his uncles, Richard Wordsworth, and Christopher Crackanthorpe, under whose care his three brothers and his sister were placed on the death of their father, in 1795. The orphans were at this time nearly, if not entirely, dependent upon their relatives, in consequence of the stubborn refusal of the wilful, if not mad, Sir James Lowther, to settle the claims of their father upon his estate.

The impressions which Wordsworth received of Cambridge, on his arrival, and during his subsequent residence in that university, are vividly pictured in the "Prelude." The "long-roofed chapel of King's College," lifting its "turrets and pinnacles in answering files," high above the dusky grove of trees which surrounded it, was the first object which met his eye, as he approached the town. Then came the students, "eager of air and exercise," taking their constitution walks; and the old Castle, built in the time of the Conqueror; and finally Magdalene bridge, and the glimpse of the Cam caught in passing over it, and the far-famed and much-loved Hoop Hotel.

" My spirit was up, my thoughts were full of hope;
Some friends I had, acquaintances who there
Seemed friends, poor simple school-boys, now hung round
With honour and importance; in a world
Of welcome faces up and down I roved;
Questions, directions, warnings, and advice
Flowed in upon me from all sides; fresh day
Of pride and pleasure, to myself I seemed
A man of business and expense, and went
From shop to shop about my own affairs,
To tutor or to tailor, as befel,
From street to street, with loose and careless mind."

The University seemed like a dream to him:

" I was the dreamer, they the dream; I roamed
Delighted thro' the motley spectacle;
Gowns—grave or gaudy—doctors, students, streets,
Courts, cloisters, flocks of churches, gateways, towers;

Migration strange for stripling of the hills—
A northern villager."

And then he goes on to describe his personal appearance and habits; how suddenly he was changed amidst these scenes, as if by some fairy's wand; rich in monies, and attired—

"In splendid garb, with hose of silk, and hair
Powdered, like rimy trees when frost is keen;
My lordly dressing-gown, I pass it by,
With other signs of manhood, that supplied
The lack of beard.—The weeks went roundly on;
With invitations, suppers, wine, and fruit;
Smooth housekeeping within—and all without
Liberal, and suiting gentlemen's array."

The contrast is picturesque and striking enough of Wordsworth, the Hawkshead schoolboy, clad in rustic garb, and placed under the control of his good dame, in her little whitewashed cottage, with its warm peat-fire; to Wordsworth, the collegian, dressed in silk-stockings, with his powdered hair, plentiful monies, troops of wine-drinking, and sight-loving friends. Perhaps, it was natural that Wordsworth should be proud of his butterfly-wings, after having escaped from the shell of the chrysallis—but no one could have imagined, from the grave, high, and austere character he afterwards sustained, that he had, at any previous time of his life, given way to the weakness of dandyism. Youth, however, is not to be measured by severe standards; and even if it were to be so measured, Wordsworth has not many sins to answer for, and certainly none of a venial cast. He was, nevertheless, what would be called a gay young fellow, during the first year of his college life; and he himself attributes a good deal of this to the fact that he was before the freshmen of his year in Latin and mathematics, and had, therefore, no pressing inducement to study. Pleasure called him with her syren voice, and he, nothing loath, obeyed her behests. Still he did not neglect his studies; although French and Italian, with the literature of his own country, seem to be the staple of the scholarship he acquired at Cambridge. "It is true," says De Quincy, " that he took the regular degree of B.A., and in the regular course; but this was won in those days by a mere nominal examination, unless where the mathematical attainments of the student prompted his ambition to contest the honourable distinction of Senior Wrangler. This, in common with all other honours of the university, is won, in our days, with far severer effort than in that age of relaxed discipline; but at no period could it have been won, let the malicious and the scornful say what they will, without an amount of mathematical skill very much beyond what has ever been exacted of its *alumni* by any other European university. Wordsworth was a professed admirer of the mathematics; at least of the higher geometry. The secret of this admiration for geometry lay in the antagonism between this world of bodiless abstraction and the world of passion."

Leaving this subject of his attainments, however, and returning to his college life, it may farther be stated, as a proof of Wordsworth's love of good fellowship at this time, that during a visit to a friend who occupied the rooms which John Milton, the blind old Homer of the Commonwealth occupied, during his residence in Cambridge, he drank so copiously in his enthusiasm and reverence for the place, and its grand and golden memories, that he was fairly carried away on the other side of the rational barriers, and in short got gloriously drunk; not so drunk, however, that he could not attend the chapel service, and behave there with due decorum. Speaking of the great men who had trod the streets of Cambridge and worn an university gown before him, and of his great reverence for them, he has occasion to introduce Milton, and alludes to this excess at the close of the passage. I will quote it entire.

"Beside the pleasant mill of Trumpington,
  I laughed with Chaucer in the hawthorn shade;
  Heard him, while birds were warbling, tell his tales
  Of amorous passion. And that gentle bard,
  Chosen by the muses for their page of state!—
  Sweet Spenser, moving through his clouded heaven
  With the moon's beauty, and the moon's soft pace,
  I called him brother, Englishman, and friend.
Yea our blind poet, who in his later day,
Stood almost single, uttering odious truth—
Darkness before, and danger's voice behind.
Soul awful,—if the earth has ever lodged
An awful soul—I seem'd to see him here
Familiarly, and in his scholar's dress,
Bounding before me, yet a stripling youth—
A boy, no better, with his rosy cheek
Angelical, keen eye, courageous look,
And conscious step of purity and pride.
Among the band of my compeers was one
Whom chance had stationed in the very room

Honoured by Milton's name. O temperate bard!
Be it confest, that for the first time, seated
Within thy innocent lodge and oratory,
One of a festive circle, I poured out
Libations to thy memory, drank, till pride
And gratitude grew dizzy in a brain
Never excited by the fumes of wine
Before that hour, or since. Then forth I ran
From the assembly; through a length of streets
Ran, ostrich like, to reach our chapel door
In not a desperate or opprobrious time,
Albeit long after the importunate bell
Had stopped, with wearisome Cassandra voice
No longer haunting the dark winter night.
Call back, O friend! a moment to thy mind,
The place itself, and fashion of the rites.
With careless ostentation shouldering up
My surplice, through the inferior throng I clove
Of the plain Burghers, who, in audience stood
On the last skirts of their permitted ground,
Under the pealing organ. Empty thoughts!
I am asham'd of them; and that great bard
And thou, my friend! who in thy ample mind
Hast placed me high above my best deserts,
Ye will forgive the weakness of that hour,
In some of its unworthy vanities,
Brother to many more."

It is interesting to know all this—to be assured that although Wordsworth was in after life as temperate as Milton—drinking nothing but water, and requiring, indeed, no stimulants but that which healthy and robust exercise afforded—I say it is pleasant to be assured that once in his life our poet did really link himself with the imperfections of man, and by an excess of sympathy got drunk—or as De Quincy calls it, "boozy,"—to the honour and glory of Milton. It is a thing to be pardoned, and is almost the only anecdote of Wordsworth which possesses a really human interest.

The rooms which Wordsworth occupied at St. John's were so situated, that had he been a hard student instead of a gay gownsman, the circumstances which environed them might very materially have affected his studies; for immediately below him ran the great college kitchen, which was continually in an uproar of dissonance with the voices of cooks, and their preparations for the eating necessities of the college members. To atone, however, for this animal riot, the poet could look forth from his pillow by the light

"Of moon or favouring stars,"

and there behold through the majestic windows of Trinity Chapel, the pale statue

> "Of Newton with his prism and silent face,
> The marble index of a mind for ever
> Voyaging through strange seas of thought, alone."

It must not be supposed, however, from what has now been stated respecting the *gay* life of Wordsworth, that he committed any of those excesses which are so common to the undergraduates of Cambridge. He was not a Barnwell-man, nor a Newmarket jockey, nor a gambler, nor gay, indeed, at all, in the gross meaning of that word. He was more idle and genial than this; and a lover of generous society. It was not in his nature, which was always high and pure, and which had been strengthened and solemnised by his converse with the majestic scenery of his childhood,—to descend to the low forms of vice; on the contrary, he had always a dread, horror, and loathing for vice, and vicious society. And, perhaps, one primal cause of his carelessness at Cambridge, lay in his contempt for its scholastic discipline, and for the character and conduct of its chiefs and professors. He felt that Cambridge could teach him but little—that he was "not for that hour, or that place," as he himself expresses it; but for quite another hour and another place. The dead, cold formality of its religious services,—the absence from chapel of those who "ate the bread of the founders of the colleges, and had sworn to administer faithfully their statutes;" whilst the students were required, under penalties, to attend the senseless mummery;—all these things, and others, revolted Wordsworth's mind against them, and made him regard the whole system, of which they were part, with distrust and abhorrence. He thus alludes to these matters in the "Prelude:"—

" —— Spare the house of God. Was ever known
The witless shepherd who persists to drive
A flock that thirsts not to a pool disliked?
A weight must surely hang on days begun
And ended with such mockery. Be wise,
Ye Presidents and Deans, and, till the spirit
Of ancient times revive, and truth be trained
At home in pious service, to your bells
Give seasonable rest, for 'tis a sound
Hollow as ever vexed the tranquil air;

> And your officious doings bring disgrace
> On the plain steeples of our English church,
> Whose worship, 'mid remotest village trees,
> Suffers for this."

Wordsworth felt this, at the time, very keenly, and saw what a grist it afforded for the grinding ridicule of the scoffer and the atheist. Turning from these melancholy reflections, to the dear old times, when men of learning were really pious, and devoted to their scholarly functions, when

> "Bacon, Erasmus, or Melancthon read
> Before the doors or windows of their cells,
> By moonshine, thro' mere lack of taper-light,"

he conjures up a vision of scholastic life—a vision of the future—which however, he says, "fell to ruin round him," and was all in vain.

Notwithstanding the confusion of his outer circumstances, and the general aimless tenor of his life, Wordsworth did not entirely neglect his own culture—and in the silence of the academic groves, by the sweetly remembered Cam, or in his own rooms in the Gothic court of St. John's, he brooded over the problems of life, death, and immortality. The ghosts of the mighty dead haunted him likewise, as he walked through the familiar places, where they were wont to walk whilst dwelling in their earthly tenements, and roused him, at times, to commence anew the race of learning and distinction.

> "I could not always pass
> Thro' the same gateways, sleep where they had slept,
> Wake where they waked, range that enclosure old,
> That garden of great intellects, undisturbed."

And yet, with the exception of "Lines written whilst sailing up the Cam," Wordsworth does not seem to have composed a line at Cambridge. He was learning, however, the first lessons of worldly wisdom all this time; was initiated into the ways of life, and the characters of men; and such discipline could not have been spared the poet, without loss to him. He does not regret, he says, any experience in his college life, and thinks the gowned youth who only misses what he missed, and fell no lower than he fell, is not a very hopeless character.

SUMMER HOLIDAYS.

At length the long vacation, which the good Alma Mater allows for the refreshment of the minds and bodies of her dear children, came to set Wordsworth at liberty; and, in the summer of 1788, he revisited his native scenes at Esthwaite. The old cramp of University life, with its dissipations, and frivolous pleasures, fell from him like an evil enchantment, the first moment when he beheld the bed of Windermere,

> "Like a vast river stretching in the sun.
> With exultation at my feet I saw
> Lake, islands, promontories, gleaming bays,
> A universe of Nature's finest forms,
> Proudly revealed with instantaneous burst,
> Magnificent, and beautiful, and gay.
> I bounded down the hill, shouting amain
> For the old ferryman; to the shout the rocks

> Replied; and when the Charon of the flood
> Had stay'd his oars, and touched the jutting pier,
> I did not step into the well-known boat
> Without a cordial greeting."

There is something very delightful and refreshing in this burst of enthusiasm, and it shews clearly enough, which was the University Wordsworth loved best. At Cambridge he was a prisoner, with his dark heart yearning for the sunshine of his native hills; but here he was free, his heart no longer dark nor sad, but flooding with light and joy, and exulting in the delicious beauty of Nature.

And what strikes me as very touching and beautiful in the poet's relation of this visit to his birthplace, is the fact that he did not forget his old dame,—although certain critics have of late declared that he had no heart,—but that on the contrary he went straight to her cottage, and so closed his journey from Cambridge. Hear how he speaks of her and her reception of him:

> " Glad welcome had I, with some tears, perhaps,
> From my old dame, so kind and motherly,
> While she perused me with a parent's pride.
> The thoughts of gratitude shall fall like dew

Upon thy grave, good creatnre! While my heart
Can beat, never will I forget thy name.
Heaven's blessings be upon thee where thou liest
After thy innocent and busy stir
In narrow cares, thy little daily growth
Of calm enjoyment, after eighty years,
And more than eighty of untroubled life,
Childless; yet, by the strangers to thy blood
Honoured with little less than filial love."

Such is the affectionate tribute which Wordsworth pays to her memory. And if the reader be anxious to know all the small and large delights which the poet felt in renewing his acquaintance with the scenes of his childhood, I must refer him to the "Prelude." He will there read how the old dame led him—he "willing, nay, wishing to be led," through the village and its neighbourhood. How each face of the ancient neighbours was like a volume to him; how he hailed the labourers at their work " with half the length of a long field between," how he shook hands with his quondam schoolfellows; proud and yet ashamed of his fine Cambridge clothes, doing everything in the way of recognition, in short, which a kind generous, and loving heart could dictate. The brook in the garden, which had been imprisoned there until it had lost its voice—he hailed also, with the delight of many remembrances, and much present pleasure. And then how his heart overflows at the sight of his favourite dog—the rough terrier of the hills—an inmate of the dame's cottage by ancient right!—a brave fellow, that could hunt the badger, or unearth the fox—making no bones about either business. The poet slept, too, during this visit, in his old sleeping room;

> "That lowly bed, where I had heard the wind
> Roar, and the rain beat hard, where I so oft
> Had lain awake on summer nights to watch
> The moon in splendour couched among the leaves
> Of a tall ash that near our cottage stood;
> Had watch'd her with fixed eyes, while to and fro
> In the dark summit of the waving tree
> She rock'd with every impulse of the breeze."

The poet then describes the refreshing influence which Nature spread, like a new element of life, over his spirit, and quotes even the time and place—viz., one evening at sunset, when taking his first walk, these long months, round the lake of Esthwaite, when his soul

> "Put off her veil, and self-transmuted, stood
> Naked in the presence of her God;"

whilst a comfort seemed to "touch a heart that had not been disconsolate;" and "strength came where weakness was not known to be—at least not felt." Then he took the balance, and weighed himself:

> "Conversed with promises, had glimmering views
> How life pervades the undecaying mind;
> How the immortal soul, with godlike power
> Informs, creates, and thaws the deepest sleep
> That time can lay upon her; how on earth
> Man, if he do but live within the light
> Of high endeavours, daily spreads abroad,
> His being armed with strength that cannot fail."

Here was evidence that the soul of the poet was settling down, if we may say so, to something like repose, preparatory to the grand aim and purpose of his life. He begins to see that idleness and pleasure will not last—will not serve any end in the world; and that man must be a worker, with high endeavours, if he is indeed to be or do anything worthy of a man.— And this light breaking in upon him, through the twilight of Nature and his own soul, is soothing, consolatory, and hopeful to him. He begins, likewise, to take a fresh interest in the daily occupations of the people around him; read the opinions and thoughts of these plain living people, "now observed with clearer knowledge;" and saw "with another eye" "the quiet woodman in the woods," and the shepherd roaming over the hills. His love for the grey-headed old dame returns to him again and again in these latter pages of the "Prelude," and he pictures her as a dear object in the landscape, as she goes to church,

>――"Equipped in monumental trim;
>Short velvet cloak, (her bonnet of the like,)
>A mantle, such as cavaliers
>Wore in old time."

And then her

>――" smooth domestic life,
>Affectionate, without disquietude,
>Her talk, her business pleased me, and no less
>Her clear, though shallow stream of piety,
>That ran on Sabbath days a fresher course;
>With thoughts unfelt till now, I saw her read
>Her Bible on hot Sunday afternoons,
>And loved the book, when she had dropped asleep,
>And made of it a pillow for her head."

It would be impossible to follow the poet in

all those minute relations of incident and feeling which run throughout the "Prelude," during this first vacation amongst the hills.— One anecdote, however, must be told, for it is an inlet into the poet's nature, and shewed that he had a heart, and deep sympathies also for suffering and poverty, let the critics say what they will.

During the autumn, while Wordsworth was wandering amidst the hills round Windermere, —with no living thing in sight, and breathless silence over all,—he was suddenly startled by the appearance of an uncouth shape, in a turning of the road. At first he was a little timid, and perhaps alarmed, for it was close to him, and he knew not what to make of it. The dusky light of the evening increased the mystery, and Wordsworth retreated noiselessly under the shadow of a thick hawthorn, that he might watch it unobserved. It turned out to be a poor wanderer, of tall stature,

> "A span above man's common measure, tall,
> Stiff, lank, and upright; a more meagre man
> Was never seen before, by day or night.
> Long were his arms, pallid his hands; his mouth

Looked ghastly in the moonlight; from behind
A mile-stone propped him up."

He wore a faded military garb, and was quite alone—

"Companionless,
No dog attending, by no staff sustained,
He stood, and in his very dress appeared
A desolation, a simplicity,
To which the trappings of a gaudy world
Make a strange back-ground."

Presently, he began to mutter sounds as of pain, or birth-pangs of uneasy thought,—

"Yet still his form
Kept the same awful steadiness; at his feet
His shadow lay, and moved not."

Wordsworth now came from his hiding place, and hailed the poor, lone, desolate, old man, who rose, slowly, from his resting place,

"and with a lean and wasted arm,
Returned the salutation; then resumed
His station, as before."

The poet entered into conversation with him,

and asked him to relate his history. It was the old tale—told with a quiet uncomplaining voice, a stately air of mild indifference. He had served in the Tropic islands, and on landing, three weeks ago, he had been dismissed the service. He was now journeying homeward, to lay his weary bones in the churchyard of his native village. Wordsworth was touched at the uncomplaining misery of the poor old man, and invited him to go with him. The veteran picked up his staff from the shadowy ground, and walked by the poet's side down into the valley, where a hospitable cottage was soon found, and the soldier bestowed for the night. On leaving him, Wordsworth

> " entreated that, henceforth,
> He would not linger in the public ways,
> But ask for timely furtherance and help,
> Such as his state required."

And now, mark the touching reply of the friendless old man:

> " With the same ghastly mildness in his look
> He said, " My trust is in the God of heaven,
> And in the eye of him who passes me."

And in this manner, — with occasional adventures, but none so memorable as this,— Wordsworth passed his vacation. Nature, too, had claimed him for her own—for her bard, minister, and interpreter; had purified him of the frivolities which had previously lowered his mind, and loosed the girds of his gigantic spirit, and she now made him happy in the consciousness of his destiny. During one of his morning walks, he thus describes this consciousness:—

> "My heart was full; I made no vows, but vows
> Were then made for me; bond unknown to me
> Was given, that I should be; else sinning greatly,
> A dedicated spirit. On I walked
> In thankful blessedness, which yet survives."

Subsequent portions of his vacations were spent in Wales, and Penrith, on the southern border of Cumberland. His mother's relations resided at this latter town, and it was with them that his beloved sister Dorothy was placed when the poet's family was broken up. It was the daughter of these relations also to whom the poet was married in after life. Her name was Mary Hutchinson; she was a schoolmate of the poet's at Penrith, and an affectionate, intelligent, good wife she made him, during the forty-eight years of their wedded life. And now, during the holidays, these beautiful persons—viz. Dorothy and Mary, were his companions, as he roved amongst the scenery of Penrith.*" He mounted with them the Border Beacon, on the north-east of the town; and, on that eminence, now overgrown with fir trees, which intercept the view, but which was then free and open, and displayed a glorious panorama, he beheld the wide plain stretched far and near below, closed by the dark hills of Ullswater on the west, and by the dim ridges of Scotland on the north. The road from Penrith towards Appleby, on the south-east, passes, at about a mile's distance, the romantic ruins of that

> " Monastic castle mid tall trees,
> Low standing by the margin of the stream,"

where the river Lowther flows into the Emont, which descends from the lake of Ullswater through a beautiful and fertile valley, in which

*Dr. Wordsworth's Memoir, page 53.

at the village of Sockbridge, some of Wordsworth's ancestors lived, and where, at the church of Burton, some of them lie buried. That "monastic castle" is Brougham Castle, a noble and picturesque ruin. This was a favourite resort of the youthful poet and his sister.

> "Those mouldering towers
> Have seen us side by side, when having clomb
> The darksome windings of a broken stair,
> And crept along a ridge of fractured wall,
> Not without trembling, we in safety looked
> Forth, through some Gothic window's open space,
> And gather'd with one mind a rich reward
> From the far stretching landscape, by the light
> Of morning beautified, or purple eve."

In aftertimes this castle was to be the subject of one of his noblest lyrical effusions. "The Song at the Feast of Brougham Castle."

> "High in the breathless hall the minstrel sate,
> And Emont's murmur mingled with the song."

A little beyond the castle, by the roadside, stands the Countess' Pillar, a record of filial affection, and Christian charity to which also he has paid a poetical tribute; and the woods of Lowther, at a short distance on the south, were ever associated in his memory with the delightful days which he passed in his vacations at Penrith, and were afterwards the scene of intellectual enjoyment in the society of the noble family whose name they bear."

A remarkable man, and one connected by friendship with the poet, lived between Penrith and Lowther, at Yanwath. This was Mr. Thomas Wilkinson "a quaker, a poet, a professor of the topiarian art, a designer of walks, prospects, and pleasure grounds.

'Spade! with which Wilkinson hath till'd his land,
And shap'd these pleasant walks by Emont's side,'

and the verses which follow, will hand down the name of Wilkinson to posterity, together with that of John Evelyn, and the Corycian old man of Virgil."

Wordsworth's last college vacation was spent in a pedestrian tour in France, along with his friend Robert Jones, of Plas-yn-llan, near Ruthin, in Denbighshire. De Quincy thinks that the poet took Jones along with him as a kind of protective body-guard, against the rascality of foreign landlords, who in those days were apt to play strange tricks upon travellers, presenting their extortionary bills with one hand, whilst they held a cudgel in the other, to enforce payment. De Quincy, however, is not quite sure of this, but conjectures the fact to have been so, because Wordsworth has only apostrophised him in one of his poems commencing

> "I wonder how Nature could ever find space
> For so many strange contrasts in one human face."

Jones, however, seems to have been a scholar and gentleman; and Wordsworth frequently visited him, not only at his house, in Plas-yn-llan, but afterwards at Soulderne, near Deddington, in Oxfordshire, when Jones was made incumbent of that place. At all events, whatever sympathies—whether intellectual or those of friendship — united these college chums, it is certain that they commenced their tour together, and ended it with mutual satisfaction. They set out on the 13th of July, 1790, for Calais, *via* Dover, " on the eve of the day when the king took an oath of fidelity to the new constitution." The poet gives a highly coloured account of his wanderings through France, Switzerland, and Italy, in the "Prelude," and a chart of the entire journey, commencing July 13th, at Calais, and ending September 29th, at a village three miles from Aix-la-Chapelle, is recorded in the "Memoirs." There is likewise a letter addressed to his sister, ated September 6th, 1790, Kesill (a small village on the Lake of Constance), in which the poet describes his own feelings and reflections during this romantic journey. In this letter he says, " My spirits have been kept in a perpetual hurry of delight, by the almost uninterrupted succession of sublime and beautiful objects which have passed before my eyes during the past month." He then describes the course they took from, the wonderful scenery of the Grande Chartreuse to Savoy and Geneva; from the Pays de Vaud side of the lake to Villeneuve, a small town seated at its head. " The lower part of the lake," he says, " did not afford us a pleasure equal to what might have been expected from its celebrity. This was owing partly to its width, and partly to the weather, which was one of those hot, gleamy days, in which all distant objects are veiled in a species of bright obscurity. But the higher part of the lake made us ample amends; 'tis true we had some disagreeable weather,—but the banks of the water are infinitely more picturesque, and as it is much narrower, the landscape suffered proportionally less from that pale steam, which before almost entirely hid the opposite shore." From Villeneuve they proceeded up the Rhone, to Martigny, where they left their bundles, and struck over the mountains to Chamouny, and visited the glaciers of Savoy.

"That very day,
From a bare ridge, we also first beheld,
Unveiled, the summit of Mont Blanc, and grieved
To have a soulless image on the eye,
That had usurped upon a living thought
That never more could be. The wondrous vale
Of Chamouny stretched far below, and soon,
With its dumb cataracts, and streams of ice,
A motionless array of mighty waves,
Five rivers, broad and vast, made rich amends,
And reconciled us to realities;
There small birds warble from the leafy trees,
The eagle soars high in the element;
There doth the reaper bind the yellow sheaf,
The maiden spread the haycock in the sun;
While Winter, like a well-tamed lion, walks,

Descending from the mountain to make sport,
Among the cottages, by beds of flowers."

From Chamouny they returned to Martigny, and went from thence, along the Rhine, to Brig, where, quitting the Valais, they made for the Alps, which they crossed at Simplon, and visited the Lake Como, in Italy. Wordsworth's description of the scenery round Como, is in his highest manner :—

"The banks," he says, " of many of the Italian and Swiss lakes are so steep and rocky as not to admit of roads; that of Como, is partly of this character. A small footpath is all the communication by land between one village and another, on the side along which we passed for upwards of thirty miles. We entered upon this path about noon, and owing to the steepness of the banks, were soon unmolested by the sun, which illuminated the woods, rocks, and villages of the opposite shore. The lake is narrow, and the shadows of the mountains were early thrown across it. It was beautiful to watch them travelling up the side of the hills—for several hours, to remark one-half of a village covered with shade, and the other bright with the strongest sunshine. . It was with regret that we passed every turn of this charming path, where every new picture was purchased by the loss of another, which we should never have been tired of gazing upon. The shores of the lake consist of steeps, covered with large sweeping woods of chestnut, spotted with villages, some clinging upon the summits of advancing rocks, and others, hiding themselves in their recesses. Nor was the surface of the lake less interesting than its shores; half of it glowing with the richest green and gold, the reflection of the illuminated wood and path, shaded with a soft blue tint. The picture was still further diversified by the number of sails which stole lazily by us, as we passed in the wood above them. After all this, we had the moon. It was impossible not to contrast that repose, that complacency of spirit, produced by these lovely scenes, with the sensations I had experienced two or three days before in passing the Alps. At the lake of Como my mind ran through a thousand dreams of happiness, which might be enjoyed upon its banks, if heightened by conversation, and the exercise of the social affections. Among the more awful scenes of the Alps, I had not a thought of man, or a single created being; my whole soul was turned to Him, who produced the terrible majesty before me." From Como the tourists proceeded to the country of the Grisons; from thence to Switzerland, and the lakes Lucerne, Zurich, Constance, and the falls of the Rhine. At Basle, a town in Switzerland, upon the Rhine, they bought a boat, and floated down that glorious river, which, as Longfellow says, " rolls through his vineyards, like Bacchus, crowned and drunken," as far as Cologne, returning home by Calais.

In passing the Alps, the travellers lost their way, and were benighted. They were afterwards indebted for their safety to a peasant; and in speaking of this event, the poet has the following fine passage in the " Prelude :"—

"The melancholy slackening that ensued
 Upon these tidings by the peasant given,
 Was soon dislodged. Downwards we hurried fast,
 And with the half-shaped road which we had missed,
 Entered a narrow chasm. The brook and road
 Were fellow-travellers in this gloomy strait,
 And with them did we journey several hours,

At a slow pace. The immeasurable height
Of woods decaying, never to be decayed,
The stationary blasts of waterfalls,—
And in the narrow rent, at every turn
Winds thwarting winds, bewildered and forlorn,
The torrents shooting from the clear blue sky,
The rocks that muttered close upon our ears,
Black drizzling crags that spake by the wayside,
As if a voice were in them ; the sick sight
And giddy prospect of the raving stream,
The unfettered clouds, and region of the Heavens,
Tumult and peace, the darkness of the light—
Were all like workings of one mind, the features
Of the same face, blossoms upon one tree ;
Characters of the great Apocalypse,
The types, and symbols of eternity,
Of first, and last, and midst, and without end."

This Swiss tour furnishes the materials for many autobiographical passages in the "Prelude," which was written about ten years afterwards—and more immediately for the poem entitled "Descriptive Sketches," written in 1791—2, and dedicated to Mr. Jones. These sketches, and another poem, called "The Evening Walk," were published by Johnson, of Cambridge, in 1793. They are, according to De Quincy, who bought up the remainder, in 1805, as presents, and as future curiosities in

—" forcibly picturesque, and the selection of circumstances is very original and felicitous." I cannot speak of these poems at first hand, for they were never republished, and only a few extracts are included in the poet's collected works. De Quincy, however—himself the greatest master of our language, and the highest literary judge in Britain—is good to speak after. "The Evening Walk" is dedicated to the poet's sister, and was written during his school and college days. It is an ideal representation of the Lake scenery. The "Sketches" were composed chiefly in the poet's wandering on the banks of the Loire, 1791—2. From the specimens I have seen of them, they appear to be founded, like the earlier pieces already quoted, upon the style of Pope, though they are clothed in high and dignified language, and glow with all the gorgeous colouring which poetry can command and apply. They are totally unlike his mature poems, and have a different artistic base and execution. It will be seen from them, however, that what is called the "meanness" and "poverty" of Wordsworth's latest effusions, is not the result of incapacity, but of theoretic principle.

The "Sketches" fell into the Samuel Taylor Coleridge, in 1794, and were the means of introduction between these two great men, and of a life-enduring friendship.

"There is in them," says Coleridge, in his "Biographia," a harshness and acerbity combined with words and images all aglow, which might recal those products of the vegetable world, where gorgeous blossoms rise out of a hard and thorny rind or shell, within which the rich fruit is elaborating. The language is not only peculiar and strong, but at times knotty and contorted, as by its own impatient strength; while the novelty and struggling crowd of images, acting in conjunction with the difficulties of the style, demand always a greater attention than poetry,—at all events, than descriptive poetry has a right to claim."

Here is a specimen of this "gorgeous blossomy" style :

> " Here half a village shines in gold arrayed,
> Bright as the moon ; half hides itself in shade ;
> While from amid the darkened roof, the spire,
> Restlessly flashing, seems to mount like fire :
> There all unshaded, blazing forests throw
> Rich golden verdure on the lake below.

Slow glides the sail along the illumined shore,
And steals into the shade the lazy oar;
Soft bosoms breathe around contagious sighs,
And amorous music on the water dies."

MORE TOURS, AND FRANCE.

IN 1791 Wordsworth graduated, and left the University for London, where he spent four months; and in May of the same year he visited his friend Jones, in Wales, and made a tour through the northern parts of the Principality. A moonlight night on Snowdon is thus finely described in the " Prelude :—

"It was a close, warm, breezeless summer night,
Wan, dull, and glaring with a dripping fog,
Low hung, and thick, that covered all the sky;
But undiscouraged, we began to climb
The mountain side. The mist soon girt us round,
And after ordinary traveller's talk
With our conductor, presently we sank
Each into commerce with his private thoughts:
Thus did we breast the ascent, and by myself

Was nothing either seen or heard that checked
Those musings, or diverted, save that once
The shepherd's lurcher, who, among the grass,
Had to his joy unearthed a hedge-hog, teased
His coiled-up prey, with barkings turbulent.
This small adventure, for even such it seemed
In that wild place, and at the dead of night,
Being over and forgotten, on we wound
In silence as before. With forehead bent
Earthward, as if in opposition set
Against an enemy, I panted up
With eager pace, and no less eager thoughts.
Thus might we wear a midnight hour away,
Ascending at loose distance each from each,
And I, as chance, the foremost of the band.
When at my feet the ground appeared to brighten,
And with a step or two, seemed brighter still;
Nor was time given to ask or learn the cause,
For instantly a light upon the turf
Fell like a flash, and lo! as I looked up,
The moon hung naked in a firmament
Of azure without cloud, and at my feet
Rested a silent sea of hoary mist.
A hundred hills their dusky backs upheaved
All over this still ocean, and beyond
Far, far beyond the solid vapours stretched
In headlands, hills, and promontory shapes,
Into the main Atlantic, that appeared
To dwindle, and give up his majesty
Usurped upon, far as the sight could reach.
Not so the ethereal vault; encroachment none

> Was there, nor loss; only the inferior stars
> Had disappeared, or shed a fainter light
> In the clear presence of the full-orbed moon,
> Who, from her sovereign elevation gazed
> Upon the billowy ocean, as it lay
> All meek and silent, save that thro' a rift—
> Not distant from the shore whereon we stood,
> A fixed, abysmal, gloomy, breathing place—
> Mounted the roar of waters, torrents, streams
> Innumerable, roaring with one voice!
> Heard over earth and sea, and in that hour,
> For so it seemed, felt by the starry heaven."

This is poetry; and with the exception of the Arab and Dromedary passage, is certainly the finest in the " Prelude."

After the completion of this tour, Wordsworth was urged by his friends to take holy orders; but he was not of age for ordination, nor was his mind sufficiently imbued with love for the clerical functions at this time, even had he been of age, to have induced him to have assumed them. A Mr. Robinson offered him the curacy of Harwich, whilst he was in Wales, and the curacy was the high way to the Living. But from the above circumstances, and other motives of an active and political nature, the offer was declined, and his non-age was the apology. The truth is, that Wordsworth, like all the young, enthusiastic, and highly-gifted men of that time, was filled with the grand idea of liberty, and the hope of further enfranchisement from old forms of error and superstition, which France had raised upon the theatre of her soil. And accordingly, in November, 1791, he determined to cross the channel, and winter in Orleans, that he might watch the progress of events. He had at this time a very imperfect acquaintance with the French language, and set out on his journey alone. In that same month, France was in the convulsions of her first agony—her first birth-pangs of Revolution. "The National Assembly met; the party of Madame Roland and the Brissotins were in the ascendant; the war of La Vendee was raging; the army was in favour of a constitutional monarchy; Dumourier was Minister of the Exterior; a German army was hovering on the French frontier; popular sedition was fomented by the Girondists, in order to intimidate the government, and overawe the Crown. In the following year, 1792, the sanguinary epoch of the Revolution commenced; committees of public safety struck terror into the hearts of thousands; the king was thrown into the prison of the Temple; the massacres of September, perpetrated by Danton and his associates, to daunt the invading army and its adherents, deluged Paris with blood; the Convention was constituted; monarchy was abolished; a rupture ensued between the Gironde and the Montagne; Robespierre arose; Deism was dominant; the influence of Brissot and of the Girondists was on the decline; and in a short time they were about to fall victims to the power which they themselves had created."*

Such is a summary of the events which transpired whilst Wordsworth was in France; and he has left us a record of the hopes, and wild exultations with which he hailed the Revolution, when it first boomed above the horizon of the morning.

> "Before him shone a glorious world
> Fresh as a banner bright, unfurled
>   To music suddenly;
> He looked upon the hills and plains,
> And seemed as if let loose from chains,
>   To live at liberty."

* Memoir, page 71-2.

But, alas! the counterpart of the picture came as suddenly, not attended by the sweet breathings of a delicious music, but by the roar of mad and fiery throats, and the pageantry of blood and death. Before these dread events took place, and whilst hope was still high in the poet's heart, he made acquaintance with some of the most distinguished personages on the republican side—and, amongst others, with General Beaupuis, whom he characterises as a philosopher, patriot, and soldier, and one of the noblest men in France. At length, he stands in the midst of the Revolution; quits Orleans for Blois, and, in 1792, arrived in Paris, only a month after the horrors and massacres of September. Republicanism had prevailed—and what a republic it proved! All law and order suspended, or dead— thousands of innocent and patriotic men condemned to death on the faintest suspicions — the ghastly skeleton of Atheism seated on the throne of God—and liberty strangled in her own cradle. "What a picture," says De Quincy, " does Wordsworth give of the fury which then possessed the public mind; of the frenzy which shone in every eye, and through every gesture; of the stormy groups assembled at the Palais Royal, or the Tuilleries, with 'hissing factionists,' for ever in their centre? 'hissing,' from the self-baffling of their own madness, and incapable, from wrath, of speaking clearly; of fear already creeping over the manners of multitudes; of stealthy movements through back streets; plotting and counter-plotting in every family; feuds to extermination—dividing children of the same house for ever; scenes, such as those of the *Chapel Royal* (now silenced on that public stage), repeating themselves daily amongst private friends; and to show the universality of this maniacal possession—that it was no narrow storm discharging its fury, by local concentration, upon a single city, but that it overspread the whole realm of France—a picture is given, wearing the same features of what passed daily at Orleans, Blois, and other towns. The citizens are described in the attitudes they assumed at the daily coming in of the post from Paris; the fierce sympathy is pourtrayed with which they echoed back the feelings in the capital; men of all parties had been there up to this time—aristocrats as well as democrats, and one, in particular, of the former class, is put forward as a representative of this class. This man, duly as the hour arrived that brought the Parisian newspapers, read, restlessly, of the tumults and insults amongst which the Royal Family now passed their days; of the decrees by which his own order were threatened or assailed; of the self-expatriation, now continually swelling in amount, as a measure of despair on the part of myriads, as well priests as gentry,—all this, and worse, he read in public; and still as he read—

'his hand
Haunted his sword, like an uneasy spot
In his own body.'

" In short, as there never has been so strong a national convulsion diffused so widely, with equal truth, it may be asserted that no describer, so powerful, or idealizing, so magnificent in what he deals with, has ever been a living spectator of parallel scenes."

The reaction of the atrocities and enormous crimes of the Revolution, upon Wordsworth's mind, was terrible. But a short time before the Revolution commenced, we find him the espouser, the advocate of democracy; the enemy of monarchial forms of government, and consequently of *hereditary* monarchy; the foe, likewise, of all class distinctions and privileges; for he regarded these as enemies to human progress and happiness.— After his return to England, he says, in one of his unpublished letters to the Bishop of Llandaff, " In my ardour to attain the goal, I do not forget the nature of the ground where the race is to be run. The destruction of those institutions which I condemn, appears to me *to be hastening on too rapidly. I abhor the very idea of a revolution.* I am a determined enemy to every species of violence. I see no connection, but what the obstinacy of pride and ignorance renders necessary, between reason and bonds. I deplore the miserable condition of the French, and think that we can only be guarded from the same scourge by the undaunted efforts of good men. I severely condemn all inflammatory addresses to the passions of men. I know that the multitude walk in darkness. I would put into each man's hand a lanthern to guide him; not have him to set out on his journey depending for illumination on abortive flashes of lightning, the coruscations of transitory meteors." These were the opinions of Wordsworth before, and at the commencement of the Revolution. As I said, however, the crimes into which the leaders of it subsequently plunged, and the mad passions which influenced them, completely revolutionised the mind of Wordsworth, and filled him with the darkest forebodings. He lost for a time, his generous faith in men, his hope of human liberty, and his belief in the perfection of human nature. He has given a fearful picture of his state of mind at this period, in the *Solitary* of the "Excursion," which the reader will do well to consult. The events of the Revolution, however, brought with them much wisdom to Wordsworth. They turned his thoughts inward, and compelled him to meditate upon man's nature and destiny,—upon what it is possible for man to become; whilst they gave breadth, and depth, and expansion to his higher sympathies. From this time Wordsworth's mission as a priest may be dated. He was no longer a mere dreamer, but was deeply impressed with the stern realities—with the wants and necessities of his time; and he resolved to devote himself to the service of humanity.

In De Quincy's admirable "Lake Reminiscences," in Tait's Magazine, already alluded to, it is stated that by his connection with public men, Wordsworth had become an object of suspicion long before he left France, and was looked upon as an English spy. How little did these persons know of Wordsworth! At this very time his whole soul was in the cause for which the patriots were struggling; and his own noble heart was rendered still nobler, braver, and better, by his daily communings with the grand and sublime nature of his friend Beaupuis. To this man De Quincy pays the finest tribute of admiration and reverence which ever came from the pen of the historian, or the mouth of the orator. "This great season," he says, of "public trial had searched men's natures, revealed their real hearts; brought into life and action qualities of writers not suspected by their possessors; and had thrown man as in alternating states of society, each upon his own native resources, unaided by the old conventional forms of rank and birth. Beaupuis had shone to unusual advantage under this general trial. He had discovered, even to the philosophic eye of Wordsworth, a depth of benignity very unusual in a Frenchman; and not of local, contracted benignity, but of large, illimitable, apostolic devotion to the service of the poor and the oppressed;—a fact the more remarkable, as he had all the pretensions, in his own person, of high birth, and high rank; and, so far as he had any personal interest embarked in the struggle, should have allied himself to the aristocracy. But of selfishness in any shape, he had no vestiges; or if he had, it shewed itself in a slight tinge of vanity; yet no—it was not vanity, but a radiant quickness of sympathy with the eye which expressed admiring love—sole relic of the chivalrous devotion once limited to the service of the ladies. Now again he put on the garb of chivalry; it was a chivalry the noblest in the world, which opened his ear to the Pariah and the oppressed all over his misorganized country. A more apostolic fervour of holy zealotry in this great cause has not been seen since the days of Bartholomew Las Casas, who shewed the same excess of feeling in another direction. This sublime dedication of his being to a cause which, in his conception of it, extinguished all petty considerations for himself, and made him thenceforward a creature of the national will,—" a son of France," in a more eminent and lofty sense than according to the heraldry of Europe—had extinguished his sensibility to the voice of worldly honour : 'injuries,' says Wordsworth—

> ———'injuries
> Made him more gracious.'

And so utterly had he submitted his own will, or separate interests, to the transcendant voice of his country, which, in the main, he believed to be now speaking authentically for the first time since the foundation of Christendom, that, even against the motions of his own heart, he adopted the hatreds of the young Republic, growing cruel in his purposes towards the ancient oppressors, out of very excess of love for the oppressed ; and against the voice of his own order, as well as in stern oblivion of every early friendship, he became the champion of democracy in the struggle everywhere commencing with prejudice, or feudal privileges. Nay, he went so far upon the line of this new crusade against the evils of the world, that he even accepted—with a conscientious defiance of his own inevitable homage to the erring spirit of loyalty embarked upon that cause—a commission in the Republican armies preparing to move against La Vendee; and finally in that cause, as commander-in-chief, he laid down his life."

RETURNS TO ENGLAND.

BEFORE this last event occurred, however, in the autumn of 1792, Wordsworth had left France for London, where he remained, more or less, for upwards of a year; and it was during this time, that he wrote the unpublished letter to the Bishop of Llandaff, respecting the political opinions of his lordship, contained in an appendix to one of his sermons, a portion of which letter has already been quoted. And although Wordsworth still cleaves to his democratic ideas, and announces them fearlessly to the bishop, he by no means sympathises, as will be seen, with the mad actors in the Revolution. On the contrary, he is pained to agony when he hears of the atrocities committed in the name of liberty; and when, in the year 1794, crossing the sands of

Morecomb Bay, during one of his visits to Cumberland, he asked of a horseman who was passing, "*What news?*" and received for answer, that "*Robespierre had perished,*" "a passion seized him, a transport of almost epileptic fervour prompted him, as he stood alone upon the perilous waste of sands, to shout aloud anthems of thanksgiving, for this great vindication of Eternal justice."

Wordsworth was shocked, however, when England, after the death of the king, on January 21st, 1793, declared war with France; and now resolved to withdraw his mind, as much as possible, from the disappointed hopes which politics had brought him as their harvest, and devote himself to poetry. Accordingly, he left London, and once more commenced his ramblings, and poetic labours. He passed a part of the summer of 1793 in the Isle of Wight, hoping to find repose there; but the booming of terrible cannon, every evening, at Portsmouth, and the consciousness that a fleet was equipping in that port against France, made him sad, and full of misgivings as to the result of the enterprise. He soon left the beautiful island, therefore, and wandered, on foot, all over the vast plain of Salisbury—visiting the old and melancholy temple of the ancient Druids—and passing thence by Bristol and Tintern to North Wales. It was during this tour, on Salisbury Plain, that he commenced his poem entitled "Guilt and Sorrow;" a production of considerable vigour and ability.

Having now, in 1793, completed his twenty-third year, his friends again urged him to receive holy orders; but, feeling that he was not *inwardly* prepared for this important step, he again refused. The principle manifested in this refusal, is all the more worthy and memorable, because the poet had, at this time, no hearthstone, no place that he could call *his*. His time was employed, therefore, in travelling about, from place to place, and from friend to friend; now to good Robert Jones, in Wales,—the man whom De Quincy conjectures to have had no brains, and for which I owe the said De Quincy a grudge, notwithstanding that I think more highly of him than any other man now living in these realms,—and now to Mr. Rawson's, of Millhouse, Halifax, who had married Wordsworth's cousin, Miss Threlkeld, the lady who brought up Dorothy Wordsworth.

the dearly beloved sister of the poet. In 1794, Wordsworth writes to his friend Mathews " that his sister is under the same roof with him; but that he is doing nothing, and knows not what will become of him." All his path lay dark and gloomy before him. He was recommended to study the law, but he absolutely refused; and the Fates seemed to be sporting with him. His love for Dorothy grew in him every day, and it was in the year I am now speaking of, that she, having accompanied him by coach from Halifax to Kendal, *walked* with him from the latter place to Grasmere—eighteen miles, and from thence to Keswick—fifteen miles further, where they put up at a farm-house, called Windybrow, and became thenceforth all-in-all to each other.

But the grand question for Wordsworth now to solve was, how he should earn his daily bread. His poetry brought no grist to the mill; and he had no friends to fall back on. In this condition, he wrote to his friend Mathews, who was connected with the London Press, to get him employment upon one of the daily or weekly papers, but without success.

He projected, likewise, several literary journals, with the same bad fortune.

At last, however, Providence had ordained that a young man, named Raisley Calvert, should die, and leave the poet £900. Poor fellow! He seems to have been born for this special purpose. Wordsworth had known him previous to his illness, and the young man was so impressed with the genius and capabilities of the poet, that he bequeathed his little fortune to him, in order that he might have leisure to develope them. This was in 1795, whilst the negociations respecting the newspaper employment were still pending. It was at Mrs. Sowerby's hostel, at the sign of the "Robin Hood," in Penrith, where poor Calvert lay sick —where Wordsworth nursed and tended him, —and where also he died.

This bequest was of the last importance to Wordsworth, for it rescued him from poverty and distress, and enabled him to *live*.

All the avenues of the world were closed against him; for he was, by nature and education, unfitted for the tradesman's service, or the clerk's office, or the schoolman's desk. He was a solitary dreamer; a lonely, meditative man, who thought golden thoughts, and built starry ladders to heaven, and did all sorts of strange things, similar in character, which unfortunately could not be sold as wares in the public market-place. And it was necessary, if Wordsworth was to be any thing, that he should continue this foolish habit of dreaming, of rhyming, and writing, into which he had so singularly fallen. For in her education of the poet, Nature—who is a wise teacher and developer—always adopts one regular method, although she frequently varies the process: and this method consists in impressing the mind with her manifold forms, colours, sounds, and works, that they may hereafter be reproduced in the glorious imagination of the poet, and shine, like rich mosaics, in the wisdom of his teaching. But for the friend alluded to, however, our poet could never have afforded to have gone through his initiation in the mysteries of poetry, but must have squatted down as a school-master in some suitable town (which De Quincy says he once thought of doing), and have turned professor of flogging Greek, into pigmy humanities. Or, perhaps, the Poet of Rydal might have been little better than a *scribe-engro*, if I may coin a word from George Borrows' "Romany," and have ended his life as a political or literary hack, in some *Times'* omnibus, or other vehicle of less note and more principle.

Fortunately for literature, and for men, as the readers of literature, Raisley Calvert was born and died—and the " Excursion" was written. I would not, however, be thought to speak ungenerously of poor Calvert :—God forbid !—but still I cannot help thinking about Providence, and His dark, inscrutable ways how He smites one frail child to the grave that another may have leisure to sing songs.— The poet never forgets the bounty and generosity of the poor dead heart, now hushed to silence, but raises this monument to his memory :

> " Calvert ! it must not be unheard by them
>   Who may respect my name, that I to thee
>   Owe many years of early liberty.
> This care was thine, when sickness did condemn
> Thy youth to hopeless wasting, root and stem,
>   That I, if frugal and severe, might stray
>   Where'er I liked, and finally array
> My temples with the Muse's diadem.
> Hence, if in freedom I have loved the truth,

> If there be aught of pure, or good, or great,
> In my past verse, or shall be in the lays
>   Of highest mood, which now I meditate,
> It gladdens me, O worthy short-lived youth,
>   To think how much of this will be thy praise."

In a letter which Wordsworth wrote to his dear friend, Sir George Beaumont, Bart., in the year 1806, we learn the manner in which the £900, bequeathed to him by Calvert, were invested. " Upon the interest of the £900, £400 being laid out in annuity, with £200," says Wordsworth, " deducted from the principal, and £100, a legacy to my sister, and £100 more, which the " Lyrical Ballads" have brought me, my sister and I lived seven years—nearly eight." And it is certain that this sister, who never left him from this time through his long life, exercised a beautiful and benign influence over the poet, softened the asperities of his character, and cheered him in his despondency. He thanks God that his " beloved sister,'

> ———" in whose sight
> Those days were passed,"

maintained for him a saving intercourse with

his true self. It was to her that he was indebted for many salutary admonitions; it was she who, in the midst of the clashing politics and noisy-throated revolutions of Europe, preserved him "still a poet," and made "him seek beneath that name, and that alone, his office upon earth."

In 1795, Wordsworth, accompanied by his sister, left Cumberland, for Racedown Lodge, near Cremkerne, in Dorsetshire. The country was delightful, and the house pleasantly situated, with a garden attached to it. They passed their time in reading, gardening, writing, and in translating Ariosto, and other Italian poets. We also find the poet making imitations of Juvenal's Satires, copies of which he sent to his friend Wrangham, with a view to joint publication. They were never printed, however; and Wordsworth, in 1805, when he was urged by the same friend to allow them to appear, repudiated them altogether, and regretted that he had spent so much time in their composition, declaring that he had come to a "fixed resolution to steer clear," now and for ever, of all personal satire. During this same year of '95, he finished his poem on "Guilt and Sorrow," and began his tragedy of "The Borderers," which was completed before the close of the following year. It is a cumbrous affair, and will not act; but it contains some fine passages. It was first published in 1842, and was offered to Mr. Harris, the manager of the Covent Garden Theatre, through Mr. Knight, the actor, and was, as Wordsworth confesses, "*judiciously* returned, as not calculated for the stage"

In the year 1797, Coleridge came to Racedown. Miss Wordsworth describes him in one of her letters as " a wonderful man;" his conversation teeming with " soul, mind, and spirit," —three things very nearly related to each other, one would think. He is benevolent, too, good-tempered, and cheerful, like her dear brother William, and " interests himself much about every little trifle." At first she thought him very plain—that is for about " three minutes" for he is " pale, thin, has a wide mouth, thick lips, and not very good teeth; longish, loose growing, half-curling, rough black hair.' But he no sooner began to talk than she forgot his want of comeliness, his bad teeth, and wide mouth, and was entranced by the magic of his eloquence. " His eye," she adds, " is large and full, not very dark, but grey; such an eye as would receive from a heavy soul the dullest expression; but it speaks every emotion of his animated mind; it has more of the 'poet's eye in a fine frenzy rolling,' than I ever witnessed. He has fine dark eye-brows, and an overhanging forehead."

Such was the apparition of Coleridge, in Wordsworth's house at Racedown. The poet himself was delighted with his visitor, and they were soon in deep conversation about literature, and their own several adventures, and proposed argosies on that great and shoreless deep.—Wordsworth read a new poem, which he had just written, called the "Ruined Cottage,"—and Coleridge praised it highly. Then they sat down to tea, and presently the latter "repeated two acts and a half of his tragedy, 'Osoris.'"

The next morning, the "Borderers" was read, and passages from "twelve hundred lines of blank verse,—superior," says Coleridge, in a letter to a friend, "I hesitate not to aver, to anything in our language which in any way resembles it." "I speak with heart-felt sincerity, and I think combined judgment, when I tell you," he elsewhere writes, "that I feel a little man by his side."

Coleridge came several times to see his big man, after this; and the two poets grew so much attached to each other, and found such profitable advantages in each other's conversation and literary judgments, that they resolved to dwell nearer to each other. Accordingly Wordsworth and his sister went to live at Alfoxden, near Stowey, where Coleridge was residing. This was in. July, 1797,—and he describes his sojourn there as a very "pleasant and productive time of his life." The house which Wordsworth occupied belonged to Mr. St. Aubyn, who was a minor,—and the condition of occupancy seems to have been, that the poet should keep the house in repair.

In one of Miss Wordsworth's letters, dated August 14, 1797, she speaks with great enthusiasm and delight, both of the house and the country. "Here we are," she says, "in a large mansion, in a large park, with seventy head of deer around us. . . . . Sea, woods wild as fancy ever painted, brooks clear and pebbly as in Cumberland, villages so romantic, &c. The woods are as fine as those at Lowther, and the country more romantic; it has the character of the less grand part of the neighbourhood of the Lakes." She then describes their "favourite parlour," which, like that of Racedown, looks into the garden. They were three miles from Stowey, and only two from the sea. Look which way they would, their eyes were filled with beauty: smooth downs, and valleys with small brooks running down them, through green meadows, hardly ever intersected with hedges, but scattered over with trees. The hills were covered with bilberries, or oak woods. They could walk for miles over the hill-tops, which was quite smooth, without rocks.

And in this beautiful locality did the poet reside for about twelve months, composing during that time, all the poems contained in the first edition of the " Lyrical Ballads,' with the exception of the " Female Vagrant." These *Ballads* are in many ways remarkable : in the first place, because they were the joint production of men who subsequently proved themselves to be two of our greatest poets; and, secondly, because they brought these men prominently before the eyes of the public and of the critical world. The Ballads, as they were called, were likewise of a very high order; and it is not too much to say, that such a book of poems as this had not been published since the Augustan era of our literature, Milton's alone excepted, if Milton may not be said to have closed that era. Here first appeared the "Ancient Mariner," and the "Nightingale," by Coleridge; "Tintern Abbey," and "Lines left under a Yew-tree Seat," by Wordsworth; four poems which of themselves were sufficient to float half a dozen volumes. It is true that the "Ancient Mariner," the "*Old Navigator*," as Coleridge loved to call it, is what may be styled a *made-up* poem—a wild, unearthly patch-work of the imagination,— but it contains, nevertheless, such passages as it would be rare to match outside those seas. It is full, too, of all kinds of music—sweet, wild, natural, and supernatural—now grand, like the rolling bass of some mighty organ, and now, ærial, celestial; catching up the reader into a strange heaven, and filling him with an unspeakable ecstacy. Wonderful power is likewise manifested in the structure of the tale; and one is amazed how so slender an incident, as that upon which the tale is founded, could be worked out so successfully, and with such deep and thrilling interest. The "Nightingale," however, is quite a different poem, and is redolent of nature. "Tintern Abbey," and "Lines left under a Yew-tree Seat," are in Wordsworth's best style, and have never been surpassed by him, in the fullest maturity of his genius.

The idea of the "Ballads" originated in the following circumstances: Wordsworth and his sister, accompanied by Coleridge, commenced a pedestrian tour, in November 1797, to Linton, and the Valley of Stones, near it. The whole party, however, were so poor that they could ill afford the expense of the journey, and the two poets resolved to write a poem for the "New Monthly Magazine," for which they hoped to get £5, and thus balance the outlay which they required for the tour. The course of the friends lay along the Quartock Hills, towards Watchet; and here it was that Coleridge planned his "Old Navigator," the base of it being, as he said, a dream of Cruikshanks'. Wordsworth and Coleridge were to have written this poem conjointly, but the great dissimilarity of their manner soon compelled them to abandon this idea, and Coleridge was left to complete the work by himself. Wordsworth suggested, however, as some crime was to be committed by the Mariner, which was to bring upon him a spectral persecution in his wanderings, as the consequence of that crime, that he should be represented as having killed an Albatross on entering the South-Sea, and that the tutelary spirits of these regions should follow him and avenge the crime. The navigation of the ship by the dead men was also a suggestion of Wordsworth's. As Coleridge proceeded with his work, it was very soon found that it would be too long for the Magazine, and they began to think of issuing it as a volume, along with other poems, by both bards. These poems were to be founded " on supernatural subjects, taken from common life, but to be looked at, as much as might be, through an imaginative medium." Wordsworth's share in the poetical contributions to this volume, besides those already mentioned were, amongst others, "The Idiot Boy," "Her Eyes are Wild," " We are Seven," and " The Thorn." The last verse of " We are Seven," was composed first, and Coleridge threw off, impromptu, the first verse of the poem, whilst the little party were sitting down to tea, in the pretty little parlour at Alfoxden, which looked out into the garden. Speaking of the "Idiot Boy," Wordsworth says: —" The last stanza, 'The cocks did crow, and moon did shine so cold,' was the production of the whole. The words were reported to me by my dear friend Thomas Poole; but I have since heard the same reported of other idiots. Let me add, that this long poem was composed in the groves of Alfoxden, almost extempore; not a word, I believe, being corrected, though one stanza was omitted. I mention this in gratitude to those happy moments, for in truth I never wrote anything with so much glee."

It was in 1798 that the Lines to Tintern Abbey were written. The poet and his sister had been staying for a week with Mr. Cottle, of Bristol, visiting Coleridge by the way, who had a little time before resigned his ministerial engagement with a Unitarian congregation at Bristol, and was now in receipt of an annuity of £150, given to him by the magnificent generosity of " Josiah and Thomas Wedgwood." From Mr. Cottle's they proceeded to the Banks of the Wye, crossed the Severn ferry, and walked ten miles further to Tintern Abbey, a very beautiful ruin on the Wye. They proceeded, next morning, along the river, through Monmouth, to Goderich Castle, returning to Tintern in a boat, and from thence in a small vessel back again to Bristol.

"The Wye," says Wordsworth, "is a stately and majestic river, from its width and depth, but never slow and sluggish—you can always hear its murmur. It travels through a woody country, now varied with cottages and green meadows, and now with huge and fantastic rocks. . . . . No poem of mine was composed under circumstances more pleasant for me to remember than this [viz., "Tintern Abbey:"]— I began it upon leaving Tintern, after crossing the Wye, and concluded it just as I was entering Bristol, in the evening, after a ramble of four or five days with my sister. Not a line of it was uttered, and not any part of it written down, till I reached Bristol. It was published almost immediately after in the "Lyrical Ballads."

"Peter Bell" was likewise written about this time; and the following interesting particulars, respecting its origin, are furnished by the poet:

"This tale was founded upon an anecdote which I read in a newspaper, of an ass being found hanging his head over a canal, in a wretched posture. Upon examination, a dead body was found in the water, and proved to be the body of its master. In the woods of Alfoxden, I used to take great delight in noticing the habits, tricks, and physiognomy of asses; and it was here, no doubt, that I was put upon writing the Poem of 'Peter Bell,' out of liking for the creature that is so often dreadfully abused. The countenance, gait, and figure of Peter were taken from a wild rover with whom I walked from Builth, on the river Wye, downwards, nearly as far as the town of Hay. He told me strange stories. It has always been a pleasure to me through life, to catch at every opportunity that has occurred in my rambles, of being acquainted with this class of people. The number of Peter's wives was taken from the trespasses in this way of a lawless creature who lived in the county of Durham, and used to be attended by many women, sometimes not less than half a dozen, as disorderly as himself; and a story went in the county, that he had been heard to say, whilst they were quarrelling: 'Why can't you be quiet?—there's none so many of you.' Benoni, or the child of sorrow,

I knew when I was a school-boy. His mother had been deserted by a gentleman in the neighbourhood, she herself being a gentlewoman by birth. The circumstances of her story were told me by my dear old dame, Ann Tyson, who was her confidante. The lady died brokenhearted. The crescent moon, which makes such a figure in the prologue, assumed this character one evening, while I was watching its beauty, in front of Alfoxden House. I intended this poem for the volume before spoken of; but it was not published for more than twenty years afterwards. The worship of the Methodists, or Ranters, is often heard during the stillness of the summer evening, in the country, with affecting accompaniments of moral beauty. In both the psalmody and voice of the preacher there is not unfrequently much solemnity, likely to impress the feelings of the rudest characters, under favourable circumstances."

It was during Wordsworth's residence in the South, in 1794, that a circumstance occurred, which has not been alluded to before in these memoirs, but which is interesting in itself, and still more so from the fact that it was the means of making Wordsworth acquainted with

Coleridge, Southey, Robert Lovell, and George Burnet. I will relate this circumstance in the language of a writer for Chambers' Papers for the People, and quote still further passages from the same tract, illustrative of the life of Wordsworth and his friends, at this time.*

The circumstance was as follows: Coleridge, Southey, Lovell, and Burnet "came down to Bristol, as the most convenient part from which they could embark for the wild banks of the Susquehana. On that remote river they were to found a Platonic Republic, where everything was to be in common, and from which vice and selfishness were to be for ever excluded. These ardent and intellectual adventurers had made elaborate calculations how long it would take them to procure the necessaries of life, and to build their barns, and how they should spend their leisure in what Coleridge sung as

'Freedom's undivided dell,
Where toil and health with mellowed love shall dwell;
Far from folly, far from men,
In the rude romantic glen.'

Yet, it is supposed, they knew nothing of the

* Chambers' Papers for the People, article Wordsworth.

Susquehana more than of any other American river, except that its name was musical and sonorous; and far from having anything wherewith to convey themselves and their moveables across the Atlantic, they had to borrow five pounds to make up their lodging bill. This sum was advanced them, with unalloyed pleasure, by Mr. Cottle, a bookseller in the town, a benevolent and worthy man, who seems almost to have been located there for no other purpose than to introduce the three chief Lake Poets to the world.

"The bubble of the Susquehana, or, as it was called, Pantisocracy, was exploded, by Southey, Coleridge, and Lovell, all getting into the bonds of matrimony, which have a miraculous virtue in testing the solidity of schemes of life. They married three sisters of the name of Fricker. It was the perpetual restlessness of Coleridge which first brought him and his companions into contact with Wordsworth. The former wonderful man, in capabilities perhaps the mightiest of that illustrious group, and in his mental constitution one of the most puzzling psychological phenomena which human nature has ever presented, was the originator of the

Pantisocratic proposal. He was a man of luxurious imagination, deep emotiveness, various learning, and an exquisite nervous susceptibility. In 1795, he was making excursions through the lovely and tranquil scenery of Somersetshire, when he became acquainted with a most worthy and excellent man, Mr. Poole, resident in the quiet village of Stowey. On his return to Bristol, where he was married, he still exhibited his uneasiness. First he removed to his immortal rose-bound cottage at Clevedon, then back to the pent-up houses at Redcliff Hill, and from these again to the more open situation of Kingsdown. Nothing would then satisfy him but he must set up a serial, to be called 'The Watchman;' and his own sketches of his travelling canvass for that periodical, might take rank with some chapters of Don Quixote. Take, for instance, this picture of a great patriot at Birmingham, to whom he applies for his magnificent patronage:—He was 'a rigid Calvinist, a tallow-chandler by trade. He was a tall, dingy man, in whom length was so predominant over breadth, that he might almost have been borrowed for a foundry poker! Oh, that face!—I have it before me at this moment. The lank, black, twine-like hair, pinguinitescent, cut in a straight line along the black stubble of his thin, gunpowder eyebrows, that looked like a scorched aftermath from a last week's shaving. His coat-collar behind, in perfect unison, both of colour and lustre, with the coarse yet glib cordage which I suppose he called his hair, and which, with a bend inward at the nape of the neck—the only approach to flexure in his whole figure—slunk in behind his waistcoat; while the countenance, lank, dark, very hard, and with strong, perpendicular furrows—gave me a dim notion of some one looking at me through a gridiron,—all soot, grease, and iron.' This thoroughbred lover of liberty, who had proved that Mr. Pitt was one of the horns of the second beast in the 'Revelations' that spake as a dragon, nevertheless declined to take 'The Watchman;' and in short, after a disastrous career, that serial died a natural death. The disappointed editor took refuge, for a brief season, with Mr. Poole, at Stowey, and there, for the first time, he met Wordsworth, who then resided about twenty miles off, at Racedown, in Dorsetshire.

"Coleridge returned for a short time to Bristol, but in January, 1797, he removed to Stowey, where he rented a small cottage. This must have been a pleasant episode in the lives of the gifted individuals whom it brought together in that sweet village. Wordsworth, who was now twenty-seven, had come with his sister to Alfoxden, which was within two miles of Stowey. Charles Lloyd, a young man of most sensitive and graceful mind, and of great poetical susceptibility, resided in the family with Coleridge. Charles Lamb, then in the spring-time of his life, was also a frequent inmate; and often afterwards, under the cloud which lowered over his noble devotedness in London, his fancy wandered back to that happy valley.— Why, says he to Charles Lloyd, who unexpectedly looked in upon him in the great Babylon:

> ' Why seeks my Lloyd the stranger out?
> What offering does the stranger bring
> Of social scenes, home-bred delights,
> That him in aught compensate may
> For Stowey's pleasant winter nights,
> For loves and friendships far away?'

The Pantisocratist, George Burnet, was also a

visitor. Mrs. Coleridge herself had a poetical taste, and there is one very graceful piece of hers written on the receipt of a thimble from her kind friend Mr. Cottle. Just such a thimble, sings Sarah Coleridge—

> 'Just such a one, *mon cher ami*
> (The finger-shield of industry),
> The inventive gods, I deem, to Pallas gave,
> What time the vain Arachne, madly brave,
> Challenged the blue-eyed virgin of the sky
> A duel in embroidered work to try.
> And hence the thimbled finger of grave Pallas
> To the erring needle's point was more than callous.
> But, ah! the poor Arachne! she, unarmed,
> Blundering through hasty eagerness, alarmed
> With all a rival's hopes, a mortal's fears,
> Still missed the stitch, and stained the web with tears.'

Hartley Coleridge, the ærial child who awakened the fears and sympathies of Wordsworth, was a fine boy, rejoicing his parents' hearts; and the happy pair had cut a road into their neighbours' orchards, that they might pass to their firesides under the arches of blossoms, with a speed suiting to their affections. Alas! that sweet Stowey. Cottle, in his old age, has painted one or two pictures of it and of its gifted habitants, now in their graves, that go to the heart. Take the scene with Coleridge in the jasmine arbour, where the tripod table was laden with delicious bread and cheese, and a mug of the true brown Taunton ale. 'While the dappled sunbeams,' says the old man, calling up kindly memories, 'played on our table through the umbrageous canopy, the very birds seemed to participate in our felicities, and poured forth selectest anthems. As we sat in our sylvan hall of splendour, a company of the happiest mortals, the bright blue heavens, the sportive insects, the balmy zephyrs, the feathered choristers, the sympathy of friends, all augmented the pleasurable to the highest point this side the celestial. . . . . While thus elevated in the universal current of our feelings, Mrs. Coleridge approached with her fine Hartley; we all smiled, but the father's eye beamed transcendental joy. But all things have an end! Yet pleasant it is for Memory to treasure up in her choicest depository a few such scenes (those sunny spots in existence), on which the spirit may repose when the rough adverse winds shake and disfigure all besides.' Or take the more lively visit to Alfoxden, on Wordsworth's invitation. Away they all went from Stowey; the poet and Emmeline, Coleridge and Cottle. They were to dine on philosopher's fare—a bottle of brandy, a loaf, a piece of cheese, and fresh lettuces from Wordsworth's garden. The first mishap was a theftuous abstraction of the cheese; and, on the back of it, Coleridge, in the very act of praising the brandy as a substitute, upset the bottle, and knocked it to pieces. They all tried to take off the harness from the horse. Cottle tried it, then the bard of Rydal; but in vain. Coleridge, who had served his apprenticeship as Silas Comberbatch in the cavalry, then twisted the poor animal's neck almost to strangulation; but was at last compelled to pronounce that the horse's head must have grown since the collar was put on! It was useless, he said, to try to force so huge an *os frontis* through so narrow a collar. All had given up, when lo! the servant girl turned the collar upside down, and slipped it off in an instant, to the inconceivable wonder and humiliation of the poets, who proceeded to solace themselves with the brown bread, the lettuces, and a jug of sparkling water. Who, knowing the subsequent fate of the tenants of Stowey, would not love to dwell on these delightful pictures of their better days?

"It must not be supposed, however, that the tempter never entered into this Eden; but when he did so, it was generally through the mischief-making pranks of Coleridge, who constantly kept his friends in hot water. He and Lamb had just published a joint volume of poems, and Coleridge could not refrain from satirising and parodying their offspring in the newspapers. Take this epigram as a specimen:—

'TO THE AUTHOR OF THE ANCIENT MARINER.

> 'Your poem must eternal be—
> Dear Sir, it cannot fail;
> For 'tis incomprehensible,
> And without head or tail.'

Of course nobody could suspect Coleridge of this; and, indeed, to his infinite amusement, a vain fellow affected to hesitate about being introduced to him, on the ground that he had mortally injured him by the writing of this very epigram! But Lamb could not fail to observe the doings of the poet-metaphysician more closely, and the result was a quarrel, which induced that 'gentle creature' to send him an unnaturally bitter series of theological questions, such as—' Whether the vision beatific be anything more or less than a perpetual representment, to each individual angel, of his own present attainments and future capabilities, somehow in the manner of mortal looking-glasses, reflecting a perpetual complacency and self-satisfaction?' Troubles from without added to this confusion within. The village wiseacres, to whom the habits of Wordsworth and his eccentric friend were totally incomprehensible, had decided that they were terrible scoundrels, who required to be looked after. One sage had seen Wordsworth look strangely at the moon; another had overheard him mutter in some unintelligible and outlandish brogue. Some thought him a conjuror; some a smuggler, from his perpetually haunting the sea-beach; some asserted that he kept a snug private still in his cellar, as they knew by their noses at a hundred yards distance; while others where convinced that he was 'surely a desperate French Jacobin, for he was so silent nobody ever heard him say one word about politics.' While the saturnine and stately Wordsworth was thus slanderously assailed, his fluent and witty associate could not expect to escape. One day, accordingly while on a pedestrian excursion, Coleridge met a woman who, not knowing who he was, abused him to himself in unmeasured Billingsgate for a whole hour, as a vile Jacobin villain, who had misled George Burnet of her parish. 'I listened,' wrote the poet to a friend, 'very particularly, appearing to approve all she said, exclaiming, "Dear me!" two or three times; and, in fine, so completely won her heart by my civilities, that I had not courage enough to undeceive her.' This is all very ludicrous and amusing now; but at the time its effect was such, that the person who had the letting of Alfoxden House refused point-blank to relet it to Wordsworth. This was of course a great vexation to Poole and Coleridge, who set about trying to procure another house in the vicinity.

"But the two bards were not a subject of jealousy and suspicion to the ignorant peasantry alone. A country gentleman of the locality became so alarmed, that he called in the aid of that tremendous abstraction—the state; and a spy was sent down from head-quarters, and lodged in mysterious privacy in Stowey

Inn. The poets could never stir out but this gentleman was at their heels, and they scarcely ever had an out-of-doors conversation which he did not overhear. He used to hide behind a bank at the seaside, which was a favourite seat of theirs. At that time they used to talk a great deal of Spinosa; and as their confidential attendant had a notable Bardolph nose, he at first took it into his head that they were making light of his importance by nicknaming him 'Spy Nosy;' but was soon convinced that that was the name of a man 'who had made a book, and lived long ago.' On one occasion Bardolph assumed the character of a Jacobin, to draw Coleridge out; but such was the bard's indignant exposure of the Revolutionists, that even the spy felt ashamed that he had put Jacobinism on. Poor Coleridge was so unsuspicious, that he felt happy he had been the means of shaking the convictions of this awful partisan, and doing the unhappy man some good. At last the spy reported favourably, to the great disgust of the rural magnate who had engaged his services, and who now tried to elicit fresh grounds of suspicion from the village innkeeper. But that worthy was obstinate in his belief that it was totally impossible for Coleridge to harangue the inhabitants, as he talked 'real Hebrew-Greek,' which their limited intellects could not understand. This, however, only exasperated his inquisitor, who demanded whether Coleridge had not been seen roving about, taking charts and maps of the district. The poor innkeeper replied, that though he did not wish to say any ill of anybody, yet he must confess he had heard that Coleridge was a poet, and intended to put Quantock into print. Thus the friends escaped this peril, which was then a formidable one. Coleridge was at the time wandering about the romantic coombes of the Quantock Hills, making studies for a poem on the plan afterwards followed out by Wordsworth in his ' Sonnets to the Duddon ;' and in the heat of the moment he resolved to dedicate it to Government, as containing the traitorous plans which he was to submit to the French, in order to facilitate their schemes of invasion. ' And these, too,' says he, ' for a tract of coast that from Clevedon to Minehead scarcely permits the approach of a fishing-boat.' "

This episode brings us back to Wordsworth,

and shows, amongst other things, the reason why he left Alfoxden, although not the slightest allusion is made to this spy business, or to the Pantisocratic scheme in the memoirs of the poet by Doctor Wordsworth. The poet's removal to Bristol sometime about July, in the year 1798, was caused, according to the doctor, by Wordsworth's " desire to be nearer the printer," and he (the doctor) quotes a letter from Miss Wordsworth, bearing date July 18th of that year, in which she says, " William's poems are now in the press; they will be out in six weeks." These poems, or " Lyrical Ballads," as they were called, were printed by Cottle, of Bristol, and Wordsworth received thirty guineas as his share, for the copyright of the volume.

" At his first interview with Wordsworth, Cottle had heard some of the lyrical poems read, and had earnestly advised their publication, offering for them the same sum he had given to Coleridge and Southey for their works, and stating flatteringly that no provincial bookseller might ever again have the honour of ushering such a trio to renown. Wordsworth, however, strongly objected to publication; but in April, 1798, the poet sent for Cottle to hear them recited 'under the old trees in the park.' Coleridge despatched a confirmatory invitation. 'We will procure a horse,' wrote persuasive Samuel Taylor, 'easy as thy own soul, and we will go on a roam to Linton and Limouth, which, if thou comest in May, will be in all their pride of woods and waterfalls, not to speak of its august cliffs, and the green ocean, and the vast Valley of Stones, all which live disdainful of the seasons, or accept new honours only from the winter's snow.' The three friends did go on their romantic excursion, saw sweet Linton and Limouth, and arranged the publication of the first volume of the 'Lyrical Ballads," which we have now seen brought to their publication day, and submitted to the judgment of the public. Dr. Wordsworth, however, does not allude in the "Memoirs" to Cottle as one of their party to the Valley of Stones.

The reader of this day, accustomed to dwell with delight and reverence upon the Old Navigator, the Nightingale, Tintern Abbey, &c., will be a little startled to hear that although only five hundred copies of the Lyrical Ballads were printed, Cottle had to dispose of the greater part of them to a London bookseller at a loss, in consequence of the terrific mud-showers of abuse which the critics poured upon the poems. Nevertheless, and in spite of the failure of the adventure, as a commercial speculation, there were minds of no mean order that detected the genius which produced them. Professor Wilson and De Quincy were amongst the number of these; and the former said, in speaking of the Ballads, that a new sun had risen at midday. Hannah More, also, who, notwithstanding her own milk-and-water productions, was a woman of discernment, was delighted with "Harry Gill," and deigned to say so in the teeth of the dirty demireps that abused it. But the volume gradually sunk for a time below the public horizon, and when Cottle gave up his business, and disposed of his copyright to the Longmans of London, these publishers returned that of the Ballads as valueless, and Cottle made a present of it to its authors.

In the meanwhile, Wordsworth and his sister, accompanied by Coleridge, with the proceeds of their poetry in their pockets, went to Germany. The writer for Chambers says—

"The different temperaments of the poets displayed themselves very remarkably on the voyage. The bard of Rydal seems to have kept very quiet; but his mercurial companion, after indulging in most questionable potations with a motley group of eccentric foreigners, got up and danced with them a succession of dances, which, he says, might very appropriately have been termed *reels.* Where Wordsworth was may be conjectured from Coleridge's remark, that those 'who lay below in all the agonies of sea-sickness must have found our Bacchanalian merriment

—————"a tune
Harsh and of dissonant mood from their complaint."

One of the party was a Dane, a vain and disgusting coxcomb, whose conversation with Coleridge, whom he first took for a 'Doctor Teology,' and then for 'un philosophe,' actually outburlesqued burlesque. The astounded bard, for the first time in his life, took notes of a dialogue, of which a single sample is enough.

"THE DANE.—Vat imagination! vat language! vat vast science! vat eyes! vat a milk white forehead! Oh my heafen! vy, you're a got!

"ANSWER.—You do me too much honour, sir.

"THE DANE.—Oh me, if you should tink I is flattering you! I haf ten tousand a year—yes, ten tousand a year—yes, ten tousand pound a year! Vell, and vat is dhat? Vy, a mere trifle! I 'ould'nt gif my sincere heart for ten times dhe money! Yes, you're a got! I a mere man! But, my dear friend, dhink of me as a man! Is—is—I mean to ask you now, my dear friend—is I not very eloquent? Is I not speak English very fine?

"And so his Daneship, in this extraordinary style, went on fishing for compliments, and asking whether he did not speak just like Plato, and Cato, and Socrates, till he lost all opinion of Coleridge on finding that he was a Christian. The discarded poet then wrapped himself in his great-coat, and looked at the water, covered with foam and stars of flame, while every now and then detachments of it 'darted off from the vessel's side, each with its own constellation, over the sea, and scoured out of sight like a Tartar troop over a wilderness.' By and by he lay down, and 'looking up at two or three stars, which oscillated with the motion of the sails, fell asleep.'

"They landed at Hamburg, on the Elbe Stairs, at the Boom-House. Wordsworth, with a French emigrant, whose acquaintance he had cultivated at sea, went in search of a hotel, and put up at ' Die Wilde Man,' while the other wild man, Samuel Taylor Coleridge, strolled about, amusing himself with looking at the 'Dutch women, with large umbrella hats shooting out half a yard before them, and a prodigal plumpness of petticoat behind,' and many similar striking and unusual spectacles.

"In Hamburg the pair were introduced to the brother of the poet Klopstock, and to Professor Ebeling, a lively and intelligent man, but so deaf that they had to 'drop all their pearls into a huge ear-trumpet.' At Mr. Klopstock's they saw a bust of the poet, whom they afterwards visited. It had a solemn and heavy greatness in the countenance, which corresponded with the notions entertained by Coleridge of his style and genius, and which were afterwards discovered not to exist in the prototype himself. Coleridge, whose chief object in coming to Germany was to become acquainted with the German language and literature, left Wordsworth in Hamburg, and went to Ratzeburg, where he boarded in the pastor's house. He returned, however, for a few days, to take final leave of his friend, and the two paid a visit to Klopstock together. His house was one of a row of what appeared small summer-houses, with four or five rows of young meagre elms in front, and beyond these a green, bounded by a dead flat. The bard's physiognomy disappointed them as much as his domicile. Coleridge recognised in it no likeness to the bust, and no traces either of sublimity or enthusiasm. Klopstock could only speak French and German, and Coleridge only English and Latin, so that Wordsworth, who was accomplished in French, acted as interpreter. It may here be mentioned that this ignorance of Coleridge's brought upon him a peculiar sort of civility at Ratzeburg. The *amtmann* of that place, anxious to be civil, and totally unable to find any medium of communication, every day they met, as the only courtesy he had it in his power to offer, addressed to him the whole stock of English he possessed, which was to this effect:—

'—— ddam your ploot unt eyes, my dearest Englander, vhee goes it?' The conversation with Klopstock turned entirely upon English and German literature, and in the course of it Wordsworth gave ample proofs of his great taste, industry, and information, and even showed that he was better acquainted with the highest German writers than the author of the 'Messiah' himself. On his informing the latter that Coleridge intended to translate some of his odes, the old man said to Coleridge—' I wish you would render into English some select passages of the " Messiah," and *revenge* me of your countrymen.' ' This,' says Coleridge, ' was the liveliest thing he produced in the whole conversation.' That genius was, however, deeply moved, but could not help being disgusted with the venerable bard's snow-white periwig, which felt to his eye what Mr. Virgil would have been to his ear. After this, Coleridge left Hamburg, and resided four months in Ratzeburg, and five in Gottingen. Wordsworth had two subsequent interviews with Klopstock, and dined with him. He kept notes of these conversations, some of which are given in ' Satyrane's Letters,' in the second volume of the ' Biographia Literaria.'

One or two incidents strongly illustrate Wordsworth's peculiar character and poetical taste. He complained, for example, of Lessing making the interest of the 'Oberon' turn upon mere appetite. 'Well, but,' 'said Klopstock, 'you see that such poems please everybody.' He immediately replied, that 'it was the province of a great poet to raise a people up to his own level—not to descend to theirs.' Klopstock afterwards found fault with the Fool in 'Lear,' when Wordsworth observed that 'he gave a terrible wildness to the distress'—a remark which evinced a deep appreciation of that awful drama. Wordsworth subsequently made a short tour, and visited Coleridge at Gottingen on his return."

Wordsworth, during the greater part of his time in Germany lived at Goslar, and he found the people neither very friendly nor hospitable. Goslar is situate at the foot of the Hartz Mountains, which are covered with fine oaks and beech, and the poet and his sister, to make up for the loss of society in the town, sought solitude amongst these magnificent woods. Among the poems written at this time were, " Strange fits of passion have I known," "Three years she grew in sun and shower," "Lines to a Sexton," "The Danish Boy," intended as a prelude to a ballad never written; "A Poet's Epitaph," "Art thou a Statist?" "Lucy Gray." All these poems and many more were written in 1799; and the latter is founded on a circumstance related by the poet's sister " of a little girl, who, not far from Halifax, in Yorkshire, was bewildered in a snow-storm. Her footsteps were tracked by her parents to the middle of the lock of a canal, and no other footsteps of her, backward or forward, could be traced. The body, however, was found in the canal. The way in which the incident was treated, and the spiritualizing of the character, might furnish hints for contrasting the imaginative influences, which I have endeavoured to throw over common life, with Crabbe's matter-of-fact style of handling subjects of the same kind. This is not spoken to his disparagement, —far from it; but to direct the attention of thoughtful readers into whose hands these notes may fall, to a comparison that may enlarge the circle of their sympathies, and tend to produce in them a catholic judgment." " Lines written in Germany, '98-9" have the following note attached to them in the " Memoirs," with which I will conclude these extracts.

"A bitter winter it was when these verses were composed, by the side of my sister, in our lodgings at a draper's house, in the romantic imperial town of Goslar, on the edge of the Hartz Forest. In this town the German emperors of the Franconian line were accustomed to keep their court, and it retains vestiges of ancient splendour. So severe was the cold of this winter that when we passed out of the parlour warmed by the stove, our cheeks were struck by the air as if by cold iron. I slept in a room over a passage that was not ceiled. The people of the house used to say, rather unfeelingly, that they expected I should be frozen to death some night; but with the protection of a pelisse lined with fur, and a dog-skin bonnet, such as was worn by the peasants, I walked daily on the ramparts, in a sort of public ground or garden, in which was a pond. Here I had no companion but a kingfisher, a beautiful creature that used to glance by me. I consequently became much attached to it." During these walks he composed the 'Poet's Epitaph.' His 'Poem of Ruth,' 'The

Address to the Scholars of a Village School,' 'The two April Mornings,' 'The Fountain,' 'A Conversation,' 'Matthew,' and a variety of others were likewise written about this time. In his correspondence with Coleridge at this time, the latter speaks in terms of the highest affection for him. 'I am sure I need but say,' he writes, ' how you are incorporated with the better part of my being; how whenever I spring forward into the future with noble affections, I always alight by your side.'"

On the 10th of February, 1799, Wordsworth and his sister left Goslar, and returned towards England. The poet was now nearly thirty years of age; and as the gates of the Imperial City closed behind him, he felt like a bird suddenly released from captivity, and resolved to build up some stately architecture of verse, which men would not willingly let die. Accordingly he commenced the "Prelude," within the very hum of the city. Six out of the fourteen books which compose it, were written before 1805.

In the spring of 1799 the poet and his sister returned to England; and in a letter to Cottle, written immediately after their arrival, we find them in "the county of Durham, just on the borders of Yorkshire," thankful, after sufficient experience of Germany, for the dear face of old England once more.

GRASMERE.

THE wandering minstrel and his sister—that great-hearted, most beautiful, and devoted sister, whom we cannot help loving so devoutly, —went in the spring of 1799 to visit their friends, the Hutchinsons, at Stockton-on-Tees, and remained there, with occasional exceptions, until the close of the year. Here dwelt Miss Mary Hutchinson, for whom the poet had begun to conceive such passion as he was capable of from the time of her visit to him and his sister, at Alfoxden. For although Dr. Wordsworth is silent also respecting this visit, De Quincy tells us that it actually took place.—

And now the lovers—in their saturnine way—had leisure to cement their attachment, and what is more, they took advantage of it, as their subsequent marriage, about the commencement of the present century, sufficiently proves.—Many other things, however, occupied the poet's attention beside this, and we find him, September 20, planning another tour, and this time through the lake district, with his friends Cottle and Coleridge. It was the first time that the latter had seen the lake country, and he, in writing to Miss Wordsworth, thus speaks of it :—

"At Temple Sowerby we met your brother John, who accompanied us to Hawes-water, Ambleside, and the divine sisters, Rydal and Grasmere. Here we stayed two days. We accompanied John over the fork of Helvellyn, on a day when light and darkness co-existed in contiguous masses, and the earth and sky were but one. Nature lived for us in all her grandest accidents. We quitted him by a wild turn, just as we caught a sight of the gloomy Ullswater.

"Your brother John is one of you; a man who hath solitary usings of his own intellect, deep in feelings, with a subtle tact, a swift instinct of truth and beauty; he interests me much.

"You can feel what I cannot express for myself, how deeply I have been impressed by a world of scenery, absolutely new to me. At Rydal and Grasmere I received, I think, the deepest delight; yet Hawes-water, through many a varying view, kept my eyes dim with tears; and the evening approaching, Derwent-water, in diversity of harmonious features, in the majesty of its beauties, and in the beauty of its majesty .... and the black crags close under the snowy mountains, whose snows were pinkish with the setting sun, and the reflections from the rich clouds that floated over some, and rested over others!—it was to me a vision of a fair country: why were you not with us?"

It was in this tour that Wordsworth resolved to settle at Grasmere. First he thought of building a house by the lake side, and to enable him to do this, his brother John offered to give him £40 to buy the land. There was a small house to let, however, at Grasmere, which, after much deliberation with his sister, he finally hired, and the two inseparables entered upon it on St. Thomas's Day, 1799.

One of the very finest of all Wordsworth's letters—written to Coleridge four days after the settlement at Grasmere—details, with a graphic and truly poetic power, the wanderings of the sister and brother from Sockburn to their new home. It is too long, however, to quote here, and for a perusal of it the reader is referred to the Memoirs.*

The poet lived at Grasmere with his sister for eight years.† "The cottage," says Dr. Wordsworth, in which Wordsworth and his sister took up their abode, and which still retains the form it wore then, stands on the right hand, by the side of what was then the coach road, from Ambleside to Keswick, as it enters Grasmere, or, as that part of the village is called, "Town End." The front of it faces the lake; behind is a small plot of orchard and garden-ground, in which there is a spring, and rocks; the enclosure shelves upward towards the woody sides of the mountain above it.—

---

* Vol. 1, page 149 to 154.

† Memoirs, Vol. 1., page 156

Many of his poems, as the reader will remember, are associated with this fair spot:

> "This spot of orchard ground is ours;
> My trees they are, my sister's flowers."

In the first book of the "Recluse," still unpublished, he thus expresses his feelings in settling in this house at Grasmere, and in looking down from the hills which embosom the lake.

> "On Nature's invitation do I come,
> By reason sanctioned. Can the choice mislead,
> That made the calmest, fairest spot on earth,
> With all its unappropriated good,
> My own, and not mine only, for with me
> Entrenched—say rather peacefully embowered—
> Under yon orchard, in yon humble cot,
> A younger orphan of a home extinct
> The only daughter of my parents, dwells;
> Aye, think on that, my heart, and cease to stir;
> Pause upon that, and let the breathing frame
> No longer breathe, but all be satisfied.
> O, if such silence be not thanks to God
> For what hath been bestowed, then where, where then,
> Shall gratitude find rest? Mine eyes did ne'er
> Fix on a lovely object, nor my mind
> Take pleasure in the midst of happy thoughts,
> But either she, whom now I have, who now

Divides with me that loved abode was there,
Or not far off. Where'er my footsteps turned,
Her voice was like a hidden bird that sung;
The thought of her was like a flash of light
Or an unseen companionship, a breath
Or fragrance independent of the wind.
In all my goings, in the new and old
Of all my meditations, and in this
Favourite of all, in this the most of all. . . .
Embrace me then, ye hills, and close me in.
Now in the clear and open day I feel
Your guardianship; I take it to my heart;
'Tis like the solemn shelter of the night,
But I would call thee beautiful; for mild,
And soft, and gay, and beautiful thou art,
Dear valley, having in thy face a smile,
Though peaceful, full of gladness. Thou art pleased,
Pleased with thy crags, and woody steeps, thy lake
Its one green island, and its winding shores,
The multitude of little rocky hills,
Thy church, and cottages of mountain stone
Clustered like stars, some few, but single most,
And lurking dimly in their shy retreats,
Or glancing at each other cheerful looks,
Like separated stars with clouds between."

All this is a burst of quiet, yet beautiful, and almost ecstatic, enthusiasm—the like of which is not to be met with elsewhere, I think, in poetry. Surely, Wordsworth was worthy of his sweet cottage, and sweeter and dearer sister, and his glorious lake, with its one green island,—his mountains, and woods, and dales,—his church, and the cottages, " clustered like stars," around it; for he had the great heart, and large brain, which Nature makes the condition for all those who would share her communion. And, then, his tastes were so simple, natural, and unaffected; he lived so close to Nature, and knew so many of her secrets, and loved her too, with the passion of a first and only love. Yes, surely, he was worthy of all he enjoyed.

During the three years which elapsed, between the poet's entering upon the cottage at Grasmere, and his marriage, he was very industriously, and even laboriously, employed in cultivating his art; for he had resolved that poetry should be the business and not the pastime of his life. We find Coleridge urging him to continue the "Recluse,"—by which he meant, as Dr. Wordsworth informs us, the "Prelude;"— in the summer of 1799, and again in October of the same year, he says he will hear of nothing else but the "Recluse;' for in the mood he was in at that time, he was wholly against the publication of any small poems. He desired that his friend should build, what my friend J. H. Stirling calls an "Opus;" but Wordsworth, though still at work upon the foundations of his *opus,* cannot rest without making little oratories—holy cells—in the pauses of his labour. Hence a new volume of poems was soon ready for publication; and as the 12mo. edition of the "Lyrical Ballads," was by this time exhausted, Wordsworth determined to reprint them, and add this new volume to the work, calling the two conjointly "Lyrical Ballads, in two Volumes." The pieces now presented to the public, included some of his finest lyrical effusions. Amongst others, "Lucy Gray," "Nutting," "The Brothers," "Ruth," "Poor Susan," "The Waterfall, and the Eglantine." This new edition was published, in 1800, by Messrs. Longmans, who offered the poet £100 for two editions of the two volumes.

In 1801, Wordsworth presented a copy of the "Lyrical Ballads" to the Right Hon. C. J. Fox, accompanied by a characteristic letter; in reply to which, Mr. Fox expresses his high admiration of many of the poems, particularly of "Harry Gill," "We are Seven," "The Mad Mother," and "The Idiot Boy." Mr. Fox, however, takes exception to blank verse, as a vehicle for subjects which are to be treated with simplicity.

Other poems of deep interest succeeded these new lyrics; and I will name " The Leech Gatherer," and the " Ode to Immortality," because these poems have always been great favourites with me; and, further, because I wish to add here the notes which the poet has furnished respecting them. And first of all " The Leech Gatherer:"—speaking of this poem to his friends he says,—

" I will explain to you in prose, my feelings in writing that poem. I describe myself as having been exalted to the highest pitch of delight by the joyousness and beauty of Nature; and then as depressed, even in the midst of these beautiful objects, to the lowest dejection and despair. A young poet in the midst of the happiness of Nature is described as overwhelmed by the thoughts of the miserable reverses which have befallen the happiest of all men—viz., poets. I think of this till I am so deeply impressed with it, that I consider the manner in which I was rescued from my dejection and despair almost as an interposition of

Providence. A person reading the poem with feelings like mine, will have been awed and controlled, expecting something spiritual or supernatural. What is brought forward? A lonely place, 'a pond by which an old man *was*, far from all house and home;' not *stood*, nor *sat*, but *was*. The figure presented in the most naked simplicity possible. This feeling of spirituality or supernaturalness is again referred to as being strong in my mind in this passage. How came he here? thought I, or what can he be doing? I then describe him, whether ill or well is not for me to judge with perfect confidence; but this I *can* confidently affirm, that though I believe God has given me a strong imagination, I cannot conceive a figure more impressive than that of an *old* man like this, the survivor of a wife and children, travelling alone among the mountains, and all lonely places, carrying with him his own fortitude in the necessities which an unjust state of society has laid upon him. You speak of his speech as tedious. Everything is tedious when one does not read with the feelings of the author. The 'Thorn' is tedious to hundreds; and so is the 'Idiot Boy.' It is in the character of the old man to tell his story, which an impatient reader must feel tedious. But, good heavens! should he ever meet such a figure in such a place; a pious, self-respecting, miserably infirm old man telling such a tale!"

Having thus shown the feelings of the poet in writing "The Thorn," I will quote, secondly and lastly, the note to the celebrated "Ode." "This," he says, "was composed during my residence at Town End, Grasmere. Two years at least passed between the writing of the first four stanzas and the remaining part. To the attentive and competent reader the whole sufficiently explains itself; but there may be no harm in adverting here to particular feelings or *experiences* of my own mind on which the structure of the poem partly rests. Nothing was more difficult for me in childhood than to admit the notion of death as a state applicable to my own being. I have said elsewhere—

> " A simple child
> That lightly draws its breath,
> And feels its life in every limb,
> What should it know of death ?"

But it was not so much from the source of animal vivacity that my difficulties came, as from a source of the indomitableness of the spirit within me. I used to brood over the stories of Enoch and Elijah, and almost to persuade myself that, whatever might become of others, I should be translated in something of the same way to heaven. With a feeling congenial to this, I was often unable to think of external things as having externally existence, and I communed with all that I saw as something not apart from, but inherent in my own immaterial nature. Many times, when going to school, have I grasped at a wall or tree to recall myself from this abyss of idealism to the reality. At that time I was afraid of such processes. In later periods of life I have deplored, as we have all reason to do, a subjugation of an opposite character, and have rejoiced over the remembrances, as is expressed in the lines " Obstinate Questionings," &c. To that dream-like vividness of splendour which invests objects of sight in childhood, every one, I believe, if he would look back, could bear testimony, and I need not dwell upon it here; but having in the poem regarded it as presumptive evidence of a prior state of existence, I think it right to protest against such a conclusion, which has given pain to some good and pious persons, that I meant to inculcate such a belief. It is far too shadowy a notion to be recommended to faith as more than an element in our instincts of immortality. But let us bear in mind that, though the idea is not advanced in revelation, there is nothing there to contradict it, and the fall of man presents an analogy in its favour. Accordingly, a pre-existent state has entered into the popular creeds of many nations, and among all persons acquainted with classic literature is known as an ingredient in Platonic philosophy. Archimedes said that he could move the world if he had a point whereon to rest his machine. Who has not felt the same aspirations as regards the world of his own mind? Having to wield some of its elements when I was impelled to write this poem on the 'Immortality of the Soul,' I took hold of the notion of pre-existence, as having sufficient foundation in humanity for authorising me to make for my purpose the best use of it I could as a poet."

Now, in this note, and in the "Ode" which

it illustrates, will be found the key to all Wordsworth's philosophy, and to the secret of his mind as a poet. The mystic spiritualism which imbues all his writings, is the great distinguishing feature which marks and separates him from merely didactic and descriptive poets; and, were this element wanting in him, we should have a fine reporter of Nature's doings—a fine painter of objective effects—but no creator—no idealist, and therefore, properly speaking, no *poet*, in the high signification of that term. Luckily, however, for Wordsworth and for the world, he possessed the spiritual faculty, and kept it always active; so that his eye, even in the presence of the meanest objects, was open to the ideal things of which the symbols they were. The *infinite* was ever present to his mind, and he saw all objects through that medium of light and relationship. But the great band of critics outside the fine region in which Wordsworth dwelt, could not of course understand this "Ode," or the general tone of Wordsworth's poetry, and therefore they denounced it, as incomprehensible, mystic, and absurd. But because they had no faculty with which to appreciate spiritual representation, or even to believe in spirituality as a fact belonging to the nature of man, that was no reason in the estimation of our poet, that he should cease to sing his wonted strains in his wonted manner. In alluding to this depreciation of his poems, he very sorrowfully says, somewhere in his letters or notes, that it is a fact that " nineteen out of every twenty persons are unable to appreciate poetry ;" and we are bound to confess that this hard judgment is truth. Even the better sort of " Reviews," in which we should have expected at least a recognition of the genius and noble aims of the poet, stood out dead against him; and Jeffrey's " *This will never do,*" in speaking of " The Excursion," shows how blindly bigotted and intolerant were such critics in those days. As a sample of the abuse, and utter want of judgment which characterised Wordsworth's critics, take the following anecdotes, which are recorded by the writer on " Wordsworth," (Chamber's Tracts) as a good joke, or I will hope, as a picture of the folly of the time.

" A writer in Blackwood for November, 1829, gives an amusing sketch of a party where the 'Intimations of Immortality,' revered by the initiated as *the* 'Revelation,' was read aloud by a true disciple, in a kind of unimaginable chant then peculiar to the sect. There were one or two believers present, with a few neophytes, and one or two absolute and wicked sceptics! No sooner had the recitation fairly commenced, than one of the sceptics, of laughing propensities, crammed his handkerchief half-way down his throat; the others looked keen and composed: the disciples groaned, and the neophytes shook their heads in deep conviction.' The reciter proceeded with deeper unction, till on being asked by a neophyte to give an explanation, which he was unable to give, he got angry, and 'roundly declared, that things so out of the common way, so sublime, and so abstruse, could be conveyed in no language but their own. When the reciter came to the words, 'Callings from us,' the neophyte again timidly requested an explanation, and was informed by one of the sceptics, that they meant the child's transitory gleams of a glorious pre-existence, that fall away and vanish almost as soon as they appear. The obstinate neophyte only replied, in a tone of melancholy, 'When I think of my childhood, I have only visions of traps and balls, and whippings. I never remember being " haunted by the eternal mind." To be sure I did ask a great many questions, and was tolerably obstinate, but I fear these are not the " obstinate questionings" of which Mr. Wordsworth speaks.' This is but a small sample of the Wordsworthian scenes and disputations then of every-day occurrence. In 1816 a kind of shadow of Horace Smith again took the field. It seems that Hogg intended to publish an anthology of the living British bards, and had written to some of them for specimens. A wag, who had heard of the project, immediately issued an anthology, purporting to be this, but containing merely the coinage of his own brain. As may be imagined, Wordsworth occupied a prominent corner; and indeed some of the imitations—for most were imitations rather than parodies—did him no discredit. 'The Flying Tailor,' however, was not an infelicitous burlesque of the poet's blank verse :—

" Ere he was put
By his mother into breeches, Nature strung
The muscular part of his anatomy

To an unusual strength ; and he could leap,
All unimpeded by his petticoats,
Over the stool on which his mother sat,
More than six inches—o'er the astonished stool !"

Enough, however, has been said about these critics, for the present, at least. Wordsworth's was a struggle to get for poetry, once more, a true utterance; to annihilate the old dead, mechanical form which it had for the most part assumed, from the time of Pope downwards to him; for although Burns and Cowper had sounded the first trumpet in this morning of the resurrection, it was reserved for Wordsworth to awake the dead, and infuse into them a new and living soul.

During the residence of the poet at Grasmere, his sister kept a diary of the proceedings of their little household, which, with Wordsworth's letters, are the chief biographical records of this period, respecting the poet himself. The following extracts will give some idea of the calm and beautiful life which they led together:—

" As we were going along, we were stopped at once, at the distance, perhaps. of fifty yards from our favourite birch-tree; it was yielding to the gust of wind, with all its tender twigs; the sun shone upon it, and it glanced in the wind like a flying sunshiny shower; it was a tree in shape, with a stem and branches, but it was like a spirit of water. . . . .

When we were in the woods before Gowbarrow Park, we saw a few *daffodils* close to the water-side. . . . . As we went along there were more, and yet more; and at last, under the boughs of the trees, we saw there was a long belt of them along the shore. I never saw daffodils so beautiful. They grew among the mossy stones about them; some rested their heads on these stones, as on a pillow; the rest tossed, and reeled, and danced, and seemed as if they verily laughed with the wind, they looked so gay and glancing."

The poet was frequently indebted to this beautiful sister for the *material* of his poems; and many of the minor pieces are a musical transformation of her descriptions of natural scenery, and the feelings with which she beheld it. The poem of "The Beggars" is an instance of this; and if the reader will peruse "The Daffodils," and compare it with Miss Wordsworth's description of these fair flowers, as quoted above, he will perhaps discover how much the poet is indebted to her, in this instance also. Here is the poem.

> " I wandered lonely as a cloud
>   That floats on high o'er vales and hills,
> When all at once I saw a crowd,
>   A host, of *golden daffodils*,
> Beside the lake, beneath the trees,
> *Fluttering and dancing in the breeze.*
>
> Continuous as the stars that shine
>   And twinkle on the milky way,
> They stretch'd in never ending line
>   Along the margin of a bay :
> Ten thousand saw I at a glance,
> Tossing their heads in sprightly dance.
>
> The waves beside them danced ; but they
>   Outdid the sparkling waves in glee :
> A poet could not but feel gay,
>   In such a jocund company :
> I gazed—and gazed—but little thought
> What wealth the show to me had brought.
>
> For oft, when on my couch I lie
>   In vacant, or in passive mood,
> *They flash upon that inward eye*
>   *Which is the bliss of solitude ;*
> And then my heart with pleasure fills,
> And dances with the daffodils."

In writing to his friends the Wranghams, November 4, 1802, Wordsworth, after thanking them for their good opinion of this poem, alludes to "Butler, Montague's friend," as having said of it (the poem,) "Aye, a fine morsel this for the reviewers,"—and adds, "When this was told me (for I was not present) I observed that there were *two lines* in that little poem, which, if thoroughly felt, would annihilate nine-tenths of the reviews of the kingdom, as they would find no readers. The lines I alluded to were these—

'They flash upon that inward eye,
Which is the bliss of solitude.'"

And, now, I will make a few quotations from Miss Wordsworth's journal :—

"1802. Wednesday, April 28.—Copied the 'Prioress' Tale.' W. in the orchard tired. I happened to say, that when a child, I would not have pulled a strawberry blossom; left him, and wrote out the 'Manciples' Tale.' At dinner he came in with the poem on children gathering flowers [the poem entitled 'Foresight'].

"April 20.—We went into the orchard after

breakfast, and sat there. The lake calm; sky cloudy. W. began poem on the " Celandine."

"May 1.—Sowed flower seeds; W. helped me. We sat in the orchard. W. wrote the 'Celandine.' Planned an arbour,—the sun too hot for us.

"May 7.—W. wrote 'The Leech Gatherer.'

"May 21.—W. wrote two sonnets, 'On Buonaparte,' after I had read Milton's sonnets to him.

"May 29.—W. wrote his poem "On going to M. H." I wrote it out.

"June 8.—W. wrote the poem 'The sun has long been set.'

"June 17.—W. added to the 'Ode' he is writing ['On the Immortality of the Soul'].

"June 19.—Read Churchill's 'Rosciad.'

"July 9.—W. and I set forth to Keswick, on our road to Gallow Hill (to the Hutchinsons', near Malton, York). On Monday, the 11th, went to Eusemere (the Clarksons'). 13th, walked to Emont Bridge, thence by Greta Bridge. The sun shone cheerfully, and a glorious ride we had over the moors; every building bathed in golden light; we saw round us miles beyond miles, Darlington spire, &c.

Thence to Thirsk; on foot to the Hamilton Hills—Rivaux. I went down to look at the ruins; thrushes singing, cattle feeding amongst the ruins of the abbey; green hillocks about the ruins—these hillocks scattered over with grovelets of wild-roses, and covered with wild flowers: could have staid in this green quiet spot till evening, without a thought of moving, but W. was waiting for me . . . .

July 30.—Left London between five and six o'clock of the morning, outside the Dover coach. A beautiful morning. The city, St. Paul's, with the river—a multitude of little boats—made a beautiful sight, as we crossed Westminster Bridge [Wordsworth's sonnet "On Westminster Bridge" was written on the roof of the Dover coach]; the houses, not overhung by their clouds of smoke, were spread out endlessly; yet the sun shone so brightly, with such a pure light, that there was something like the purity of one of Nature's own grand spectacles. . . . Arrived at Calais at four in the morning of July 31st.

Delightful walks in the evening; seeing far off in the west the coast of England, like a cloud, crested with Dover Castle, the evening star, and the glory of the sky: the reflections in the water were more beautiful than the sky itself; purple waves, brighter than precious stones, for ever melting away on the sands.

August 29.—Left Calais, at twelve o'clock in the morning, for Dover . . . bathed, and sat on the Dover Cliffs, and looked upon France; we could see the shores almost as plain as if it were but an English lake. Mounted the coach at half-past four; arrived in London at six, August 30. Stayed in London till 22nd September: arrived at Gallow Hill on Friday, September 24th.

On Monday, October 4th, 1802, W. was married, at Brompton church, to Mary Hutchinson. . . . We arrived at Grasmere, at six in the evening, on October 6th, 1802."

And that the reader may hereafter have a clear perception of the persons of the poetic household at Grasmere, I will now go to De Quincy, who has drawn portraits of them, which, in the absence of any similar literary venture, are invaluable. Speaking of Mrs. Wordsworth, he says,—she was a tall young woman, with the most winning expression of benignity upon her features that he had ever beheld; her manner frank, and unembarrassed. "She was neither handsome or comely, according to the rigour of criticism, and was generally pronounced *plain-looking*, but the absence of the practical power and fascination which lie in beauty, were compensated by sweetness all but angelic, simplicity the most entire, womanly self-respect, and purity of heart, speaking through all her looks, acts, and movements. She rarely spoke; so that Mr. Slave-trade Clarkson used to say of her, that she could only say *God bless you.* Certainly her intellect was not of an active order; but in a quiescent, reposing, meditative way, she appeared always to have a social enjoyment from her own thoughts; and it would have been strange indeed, if she, who enjoyed such eminent advantages of training, from the daily society of her husband and his sister; not only hearing the best parts of English literature daily read, or quoted by short fragments, but also hearing them very often critically discussed in a style of great originality and truth, and by the light of strong poetic feeling,—strange would it have been had any person, dull as the weeds of Lethe in the native constitution of mind, failed to acquire the power of judging for herself, and putting forth some functions of activity. But undoubtedly that was not her element: to feel and to enjoy a luxurious repose of mind—there was her forte and her peculiar privilege; and how much better this was adapted to her husband's taste, how much more suited to uphold the comfort of his daily life, than a blue-stocking loquacity, or even a legitimate talent for discussion and analytic skill may be inferred from his celebrated verses, beginning:

> 'She was a phantom of delight
> When first she gleamed upon my sight;'

and ending with this matchless winding up of

> 'A perfect woman, nobly planned
> To warn, to comfort, to command;
> And yet————'

going back to a previous thought, and resuming a leading impression of the whole character—

> 'And yet a spirit too, and bright
> With something of an angel light.'"

"From these verses," continues De Quincy,

"it may be inferred what were the qualities which won Wordsworth's admiration in a wife; for these verses were written upon Mary Hutchinson, his own cousin, and his wife; and not written as Coleridge's memorable verses upon "Sara," for some forgotten original Sara, and consequently transferred to every other Sara who came across his path. Once for all, these exquisite lines were dedicated to Mrs. Wordsworth; were understood to describe her —to have been prompted by the feminine graces of her character; hers they are and will remain for ever." To these, therefore, De Quincy refers the reader for an idea infinitely more powerful and vivid, he says, than any he could give, of what was most important in the partner and second self of the poet. And to this abstract of her moral portrait he adds the following remarks upon her physical appearance. " She was tall, as already stated; her figure was good—except that for my taste it was rather too slender, and so it always continued. In complexion she was fair; and there was something peculiarly pleasing even in this accident of the skin, for it was accompanied by an animated expression of health, a blessing which in fact she possessed uninterruptedly, very pleasing in itself, and also a powerful auxiliary of that smiling benignity which constituted the greatest attraction of her person. Her eyes—the reader may already know—her eyes

> ' Like stars of twilight fair ;
> Like twilight, too, her dark brown hair ;
> But all things else about her drawn
> From May time and the cheerful dawn.'

But strange it is to tell, that in these eyes of vesper gentleness, there was a considerable obliquity of vision ; and much beyond that slight obliquity which is often supposed to be an attractive *foible* of the countenance ; and yet though it *ought* to have been displeasing or repulsive, in fact it was not. Indeed, all faults, had they been ten times and greater, would have been swallowed up or neutralised by that supreme expression of her features, to the intense unity of which every lineament in the fixed parts, and every undulation in the moving parts or play of her countenance, concurred, viz., a sunny benignity—a radiant perception —such as in this world De Quincy says he never saw equalled or approached."

Such, then, is the portrait of Mrs. Wordsworth; and now for that of sweet, musical, romantic, true and generous Dorothy. She was much shorter, much slighter, and perhaps in other respects as different from Mrs. Wordsworth in personal characteristics as could have been wished for the most effective contrast. " Her face was of Egyptian brown : rarely in a woman of English birth had a more determined gipsy tan been seen. Her eyes were not soft, as Mrs. Wordsworth's, nor were they fierce or bold ; but they were wild and startling, and hurried in their motion. Her manner was warm, and even ardent ; her sensibility seemed constitutionally deep ; and some subtle fire of impassioned intellect apparently burned within her, which, being alternately pushed forward into a conspicuous expression by the irrepressible instinct of her temperament, and then immediately checked in obedience to the decorum of her sex and age, and her maidenly condition (for she had rejected all offers of marriage, out of pure sisterly regard to her brother, and subsequently to her sister's children) gave to her whole demeanour and to her conversation, an air of embarrassment and even of self conflict, that was sometimes distressing to witness. Even her very utterance, and enunciation often, or rather generally, suffered in point of clearness and steadiness, from the agitation of her excessive organic sensibility, and perhaps from some morbid irritability of the nerves. At times the self-contracting and self-baffling of her feelings, caused her even to stammer, and so determinedly to stammer, that a stranger who should have seen her, and quitted her in that state of feeling, would have certainly set her down for one plagued with that infirmity of speech, as distressingly as Charles Lamb himself.... The greatest deductions from Miss Wordsworth's attractions, and from the exceeding interest which surrounded her in right of her character, her history, and the relation which she fulfilled towards her brother, was the glancing quickness of her motions, and other circumstances in her deportment—such as her stooping attitude when walking, which gave an ungraceful, and even an unsexual character to her appearance when out of doors. She did not cultivate the graces which preside over the person and its carriage. But on the other hand she was a person of very remarkable endowments intellectually; and in addition to the other great services which she rendered to her brother, this may be mentioned as greater than all the rest, and it was one which equally operated to the benefit of every casual companion in a walk— viz., the extending sympathy, always ready, and always profound, by which she made all that one could tell her, all that one could describe, all that one could quote from a foreign author, reverberate as it were *a plusieurs reprises* to one's own feelings, by the manifest pleasure it made upon her. ... Her knowledge of literature was irregular, and not systematically built up. She was content to be ignorant of many things; but what she knew and had really mastered, lay where it could not be disturbed—in the temple of her own most fervid heart." ... At the time this sketch was written, both the ladies were about twenty-eight years old. "Miss Wordsworth," continues De Quincy, "had seen most of life, and even of good company; for she had lived, when quite a girl, under the protection of a near relation at Windsor, who was a personal favourite of the royal family, and consequently of George the Third." Nevertheless, De Quincy thinks that "Mrs. Wordsworth was the more ladylike person of the two."

The last figure, and the greatest, in this little group of portraits, is Wordsworth's, and it is certainly hit off, like the others, with a free and discriminating hand.

"Wordsworth was, upon the whole, not a well-made man. His legs were positively condemned by all the female connoisseurs in legs that De Quincy ever heard lecture on that topic; not that they were bad in any way that would force itself upon your notice—there was no absolute deformity about them; and undoubtedly they had been serviceable legs, beyond the average standard of human requisition; for with these identical legs Wordsworth must have travelled a distance of one hundred and seventy-five to one hundred and eighty thousand English miles,—a mode of exertion which to him stood in the stead of wine, spirits, and all other stimulants whatever to the animal spirits; to which he has been indebted for a life of unclouded happiness, and even for much of what is most excellent in his writings. But useful as they have proved themselves, the Wordsworthian legs were certainly not ornamental; it was really a pity that he had not another pair for evening dress parties, when no boots lend their friendly aid to mask our imperfections from the eyes of female rigourists—the *elegantes formarum spectatrices.* .... But the worst part of Wordsworth's person was the bust; there was a narrowness and a stoop about the shoulders, which became striking, and had an effect of meanness, when brought into close juxtaposition with a figure of a most statuesque "order." ... Further on, De Quincy relates how he was walking out with Miss Wordsworth, the poet being before them, deeply engaged in conversation with a person of fine proportions, and towering figure,—when the contrast was so marked, and even painful to the poet's sister, that she could not help exclaiming : " Is it possible ? Can that be William ? How very mean he looks !" " And yet," continues De Quincy, " Wordsworth was of a good height, just five feet ten, and not a slender man ; on the contrary, by the side of Southey, his limbs looked thick, almost in a disproportionate degree. But the total effect of Wordsworth's person was always worst in a state of motion; for, according to the remark I have heard from the county people, 'he walked like a cade;' a cade being a kind of insect which advances by an oblique motion. This was not always perceptible, and in part depended (I believe) upon the position of his arms; when either of these happened (as was very customary) to be inserted into the unbuttoned waistcoat, his walk had a wry or twisted appearance; and not appearance only,—for I have known it by slow degrees gradually to edge off his companion, from the middle to the side of the high road.' Meantime his face—that was one which would have made amends for greater defects of figure; it was certainly the noblest for intellectual effect, that, De Quincy says, he ever saw. Haydon, the eminent painter, in his great picture of *Christ's Entry into Jerusalem*, has introduced Wordsworth in the character of a disciple attending his Divine Master. . . . . . " Wordsworth's face was of the long order, often classed as oval, . . . and if not absolutely the indigenous face of the lake district, at any rate a variety of that face,—a modification of the original type. The head was well filled out. . . The forehead was not remarkably lofty . . . . but it was, perhaps, remarkable for its breadth and expansive development. Neither were the eyes large, ... on the contrary, they were rather small; but that did not interfere with their effect, which at times was fine, and suitable to his intellectual character. .... The mouth and the region of the mouth—the whole circumference of the mouth, were about the strongest feature in Wordsworth's face. There was nothing especially to be noticed in the mere outline of the lips, but the swell and protrusion of the parts above and around the mouth are noticeable." And then De Quincy tells us why. He had read that Milton's surviving daughter, when she saw the crayon drawing representing the likeness of her father, in Richardson the painter's thick octavo volume of Milton, burst out in a rapture of passionate admiration, exclaiming—"This is my father! this is my dear father!" And when De Quincy had procured this book, he saw in this likeness of Milton a perfect portrait of Wordsworth. All the peculiarities, he says, were retained— " A drooping appearance about the eyelids— that remarkable swell that I have noticed about the mouth,—the way in which the hair lay upon the forehead. In two points only there was a deviation from the rigorous truth of Wordsworth's features—the face was a little too short and too broad, and the eyes were too large.— There was also a wreath of laurel about the head, which, (as Wordsworth remarked,) disturbed the natural expression of the whole picture; else, and with these few allowances, he also admitted that the resemblance was, *for that period of his life* (but let not that restriction be forgotten;) perfect, or, as nearly so as art could accomplish. This period was about the year 1807.

Here, then, thanks to De Quincy, who, for these "Lake Reminiscences" alone, is well worthy of a pension, which, had I been Prime Minister, he should have had long ago; for no living man is more deserving of this distinction for the service he has rendered to our literature:—here, I say, we have portraits of the inmates of the white cottage at Grasmere; and beautiful portraits they are. One could have wished that Dr. Wordsworth had given a little more vitality to his biography of these inmates—that he had used his pallet and brushes a little more freely (for he *can* paint, if he likes, as the description of Rydal

Mount shows); but instead of vitality, we have dry facts—which are the mere bones of biography—and these are often strung together with very indifferent tendons. We have no picture, for example, of the poet's wedded life at this time—we cannot get *behind* the scenes; all we know is, that a wedding had taken place, and the good doctor tells us, that the twain were afterwards very happy all the days of their life, just as fairy tales wind up. There seems to be a good deal of needless reserve about this matter; and I, for one, do not thank the greedy poet when he says, touching his private life, that " a stranger intermeddleth not with his joy." No one wishes to *meddle* with it; but to *sympathise* with it, and to know how this joy manifested itself in the little household, appear to be legitimate demands of the curious lovers of Wordsworth, and, indeed of all curious men, whether lovers of Wordsworth or not. But the doctor has nothing to say on these points; and all we can gather respecting them is to be found in the " Prelude," and one or two other poems. Here is the extract from the " Prelude," expressing the poet's feelings as he left the cottage with his sister before his marriage:—

> "Farewell! thou little nook of mountain-ground,
> Farewell! we leave thee to Heaven's peaceful care,
> Thee, and the cottage, which thou dost surround.
> We go for one to whom ye will be dear;
> And she will prize this bower, this Indian shed,
> Our own contrivance—building without peer;
> A gentle maid . . . .
> Will come to you, to you herself will wed,
> And love the blessed life that we lead here."

And in this place it will be well to give De Quincy's sketch of the cottage itself, where this blessed life was lived, and to share which the poet went to fetch his bride from her father's house:—"A little semi-vestibule between two doors, prefaced the entrance into what might be considered the principal room of the cottage. It was an oblong square, not above eight and a half feet high, sixteen feet long, and twelve broad; very prettily wainscotted, from the floor to the ceiling, with dark polished oak, slightly embellished with carving. One window there was—a perfect and unpretending cottage window—with little diamond panes, embowered, at almost every season of the year, with roses; and in the summer and autumn, with jessamine and other fragrant shrubs. From the exuberant luxuriance of the vegetation around it, and from the dark hue of the wainscotting, this window, though tolerably large, did not furnish a very powerful light to one who entered from the open air . . I was ushered up a little flight of stairs—fourteen in all—to a little dingy room, or whatever the reader chooses to call it. Wordsworth himself has described the fire-place of this, his—

'Half kitchen and half parlour fire.'

It was not fully seven feet six inches high, and in other respects of pretty nearly the same dimensions as the rustic hall below. There was however, in a small recess, a library of perhaps three hundred volumes, which seemed to consecrate the nook as the poet's study, and composing room ; and so occasionally it was."

So far then, De Quincy; and the following poem, already alluded to, will give an idea of the poet's feelings respecting the bride he brought with him to share the cottage blessedness of Grasmere.

"She was a phantom of delight,
  When first she gleamed upon my sight;
  A lovely apparition, sent
  To be a moment's ornament.
  Her eyes as stars of twilight fair;
  Like twilight too her dusky hair;
  But all things else about her drawn
  From May time and the cheerful dawn;
  A dancing shape, an image gay,
  To haunt, to startle, and waylay.

  I saw her upon nearer view,
  A spirit, yet a woman too!
  Her household motions light and free,
  And steps of virgin liberty;
  A countenance in which did meet
  Sweet records, promises as sweet;
  A creature not too bright or good
  For human nature's daily food;
  For transient sorrows, simple wiles,
  Praise, blame, love, kisses, tears, and smiles.

  And now I see with eye serene
  The very pulse of the machine;
  A being breathing thoughtful breath,
  A traveller between life and death;
  The reason firm, the temperate will,
  Endurance, foresight, strength and skill;
  A perfect woman, nobly planned,
  To warn, to comfort, to command;

> And yet a spirit still, and bright,
> With something of angelic light."

This beautiful poem, so full of calm affection, and intellectual homage, is a fair sample of Wordsworth's love poems, as well as a charming tribute to his wife's loveliness and virtue. In early life, it is thought by De Quincy and others, that the poet had experienced a tragical termination to an early love, and that the poems of which "Lucy" is the theme, were addressed to the object of this love; but Wordsworth always maintained a mysterious silence about the whole affair, and would never resolve the riddle of this attachment. The "Lucy" poems, however, beautiful as they are, are chiefly valuable as exhibiting the *kind* of passion which *love* showed itself in Wordsworth. Passion, in the proper meaning of the word—viz., deep, fiery, intense, and all-embracing feeling, was certainly not Wordsworth's. His love was calm, intellectual, and emotional—but it was not passion. All his love seems to have passed through his head before it touched his heart. And yet he loved his wife, and lived, as I said before, very happily with her.

Mrs. Wordsworth, however, was a true household woman, and had not acquired that faculty of walking which Wordsworth and his sister possessed, in so eminent a degree. In about a year, therefore, after his marriage—that is, August 14, 1803,—we find Wordsworth parting from his wife, and making a tour into Scotland, with his sister and Coleridge, taking Carlisle on the way. When they arrived at Longtown, they found a guide-post pointing out two roads,—one to Edinburgh, the other to Glasgow. They took the latter road, and entered Scotland by crossing the river Sark. Edinburgh was no favourite place with Wordsworth, and for reasons which are sufficiently obvious. The tourists then passed through Gretna Green to Annan, leaving the Solway Frith, and the Cumberland hills to their left hand. On Thursday the 18th August, they went to the churchyard where Burns is buried; a bookseller accompanied them, of whom Miss Wordsworth had bought some little books for Johnny, the poet's first child. He showed them first the outside of Burns' house, where he had lived the last three years of his life, and where he died. It had a mean appearance, and was in a bye situation, white-washed, and dirty about the doors, as all Scotch houses are; flowering plants in the windows. They went on to visit his grave. He lies in a corner of the churchyard, and his second son, Francis Wallace, is beside him. There was no stone to mark the spot. The greatest bard that had sung in Britain for some centuries, lay buried there like a dog. A hundred guineas, however, had been collected to build a monument over his ashes. "There," said the bookseller to the visitors, pointing to a pompous monument, a few yards off, "there lies Mr. John Bushby, a remarkably clever man; he was an attorney, and hardly ever lost a cause he undertook. Burns made many a lampoon upon him; and there they rest as you see." Yes, indeed, there they rested; and that was the deep, sad moral of the story. We shall all rest so at last. They then went to Burns' house. Mrs. Burns was not at home, but had gone to the sea-shore with her children. They saw the print of "The Cotter's Saturday Night," which Burns mentioned in one of his letters having received as a present. In the room above the parlour Burns died, and his son after him; and of all who saw this parlour on this 18th of August,—Wordsworth and his sister, Coleridge and the poor bookseller—who survives? " There they rest, as you see."

The tourists travelled subsequently through the Vale of the Nith, and crossing the Frith, reached Brownhill, where they slept.

" I cannot take leave of this country," says Miss Wordsworth, in her Journal, " without mentioning that we saw the Cumberland mountains within half a mile of Ellisland (Burns' house) the last view we had of them. Drayton has prettily described the connection which the neighbourhood has with ours, when he makes Skiddaw say—

'Scurfell from the sky,
That Annandale doth crown, with a most amorous eye,
Salutes me every day, or at my pride looks grim,
Oft threatening me with clouds, as I oft threatening him!'

These lines occurred to William's memory; and while he and I were talking of Burns, and the prospect he must have had, perhaps from his own door, of Skiddaw and his companions, we indulged ourselves in fancying that we might have been personally known to each other, and he have looked upon those objects with more pleasure for our sakes. We talked of Coleridge's children and family, then at the foot of Skiddaw, and our own new-born John, a few miles behind it; and the grave of Burns' son, which we had just seen, by the side of that of his father; and the stories we had heard at Dumfries, respecting the dangers which his surviving children were exposed to, filled us with melancholy concern, which had a kind of connection with ourselves, and with thoughts, some of which were afterwards expressed in the following supposed address to the sons of the ill-fated poet:—

"Ye now are toiling up life's hill,
'Tis twilight time of good and ill!"

During this Scotch tour the party walked through the vale of the Clyde, visited Glengyle, the scene of some of Rob Roy's exploits, Loch Lomond, Inverary, Glencoe, Kenmore, and the Duke of Athol's gardens; resting whilst in this latter place on "the heather seat which Burns was so loth to quit that moonlight evening when he first went to Blair Castle." Then they went to the Pass of Killicranky, respecting which Wordsworth wrote the following sonnet.

> "Six thousand veterans practis'd in war's game,
> Tried men, at Killicranky were arrayed
> Against an equal host that wore the plaid,
> Shepherds and herdsmen. Like a whirlwind came
> The Highlanders; the slaughter spread like flame;
> And Garry, thundering down his mountain road,
> Was stopped, and could not breathe beneath the load
> Of the dead bodies! 'Twas a day of shame
> For them whom precept, and the pedantry
> Of cold mechanic battle do enslave.
> Oh for a single hour of that Dundee,
> Who on that day the word of onset gave!
> Like conquest might the men of England see!
> And their foes find a like inglorious grave.

In the year 1803, when this sonnet was written, an invasion was hourly looked for; and Miss Wordsworth and her brother (for Coleridge had left them, worried by the " evil chance," and something worse perhaps at Loch Lomond) could not but think with some regret of the times when from the now depopulated Highlands, forty or fifty thousand men might have been poured down for the defence of the country, under such leaders as the Marquis of

Montrose, or the brave man who had so distinguished himself upon the ground where they were standing.

The tourists returned by way of Edinburgh, visiting Peebles and Melrose Abbey. Sir Walter, then Mr. Scott, was, at the time of their visit to the abbey, travelling as Sheriff of Selkirk to the assizes at Jedburgh. They dined together at the Melrose Inn. Sir Walter was their guide to the abbey, taking them into Mr. Riddel's gardens and orchard, where they had a sweet view of it through trees, the town being quite excluded. Sir Walter was of course at home in the history and tradition of these noble ruins, and pointed out to his visitors many things which would otherwise have escaped their notice. Beautiful pieces of sculpture in obscure corners, flowers, leaves, and other ornaments, which being cut in the durable pale red stone of which the abbey is built, were quite perfect. What destroyed, however, the effect of the abbey, was the barbarous taste of the good Scotch people who had built an ugly, damp charnel house within the ruins, which they called a church!

Quitting Melrose, they crossed the Teviot

by a stone bridge, and visited Jedburgh. It rained all the way, and they arrived at the inn just before the judges were expected out of court to dinner, very wet and cold. There was no private room but the judges' sitting-room, and they had to get private lodgings in the town. Scott sat with them an hour in the evening, and repeated a part of his "Lay of the Last Minstrel." Their landlady was a very remarkable woman; and Wordsworth wrote some verses expressive of the feelings with which she inspired him. Here is the burden.

" Aye! twine thy brows with fresh spring flowers,
And call a train of laughing hours,
And bid them dance, and bid them sing,
And thou, too, mingle in the ring."

Miss Wordsworth gives the following sweet picture of the home at Grasmere on their return:—

"September 25th.—A beautiful autumnal day. Breakfasted at a public-house by the road-side; dined at Threlkeld; and arrived there between eight and nine o'clock, where we found *Mary in perfect health. Joanna*

Hutchinson with her, and little John asleep in the clothes-basket by the fire."

At the ferry-house, and waterfall of Loch Lomond, Wordsworth had been struck with the beauty and kindness of two girls whom they met there, and on his return to Grasmere he wrote the following lines upon one of them :—

> " Sweet Highland girl, a very shower
> Of beauty is thy earthly dower!
> Twice seven consenting years have shed
> Their utmost bounty on thy head:
> And these grey rocks; this household lawn;
> These trees, a veil just half withdrawn;
> This fall of water that doth make
> A murmur near the silent lake;
> This little bay, a quiet road,
> That holds in shelter thy abode;
> In truth together ye do seem
> Like something fashioned in a dream;
> Such forms as from their covert peep
> When earthly cares are laid asleep.
> Yet dream and vision as thou art,
> I bless thee with a human heart:
> God shield thee to thy latest years!
> I neither know thee, nor thy peers;
> And yet my eyes are filled with tears."

This Scottish tour was a little episode in the

quiet history of the poet's residence at Grasmere. The truth is, that Wordsworth could not at this time rest long, even in his beautiful Grasmere, without the excitement of pedestrian travel and adventure. It was likewise a part of his education as a poet; the knowledge which he thus acquired of men, manners, and scenery. He had devoted himself to poetry; and every thing that tended to feed the divine faculty, he grasped at with an avidity equally as intense as that with which your mere canine man grasps at food for his perishing body. Nothing comes amiss to him; high and low, great and small; from the daffodil to Skiddaw —from Skiddaw to heaven and its hosts of glorious stars,—all are seized by this omnivorous poet, fused in his mind, and reproduced by him in song. His limited means are no barrier to his wanderings; he and his sister can live upon black bread and water, so far as rations are concerned; but setting aside the necessity of the case, this economy is for a sacred purpose,—viz. :—that they may enjoy the communion of Nature, and partake of her spiritual banquets. The gods, however, had determined to pet Wordsworth, and recompense him for his religious devotion to their doings through early life; and, to say nothing of the bequest of Raisley Calvert, the second Lord Lonsdale, just as the poet needed a wife, and larger means, paid the debt which his predecessor owed to Wordsworth's father, amounting to £1,800, as the share of each member of the family. This was a most fortunate circumstance to Wordsworth and his sister; though it mattered little to the rest, because they were well appointed in life. De Quincy says that, a regular succession of similar, but superior, God-sends fell upon Wordsworth, to enable him to sustain his expenditure duly, as it grew with the growing claims upon his purse; and after enumerating the three items of "good luck," mentioned above, he adds:— and "fourthly, some worthy uncle of Mrs. Wordsworth's was pleased to betake himself to a better world; leaving to various nieces, and especially to Mrs. W., something or other, I forget what, but it was expressed by thousands of pounds. At this moment Wordsworth's family had begun to increase; and the worthy old uncle, like every body else in Wordsworth's case (I wish I could say the same in my own), finding his property clearly 'wanted,' and as people would tell him 'bespoke,' felt how very indelicate it would look for him to stay any longer, and so he moved off. But Wordsworth's family, and the wants of that family, still continued to increase; and the next person, being the fifth, who stood in the way, and must, therefore, have considered himself rapidly growing into a nuisance, was the Stamp-Distributor for the county of Westmorland. About March, 1814, I think it was, that this very comfortable situation was vacated. Probably it took a month for the news to reach him; because in April, and not before, feeling that he had received a proper notice to quit, he, good man—this Stamp-Distributor—like all the rest, distributed himself and his offices into two different places,—the latter falling of course into the hands of Wordsworth.

"This office, which it was Wordsworth's pleasure to speak of as a *little* one, yielded, I believe, somewhere about £500 a year. Gradually even that, with all former sources of income, became insufficient; which ought not to surprise anybody; for a son at Oxford, as a gentleman-commoner, could spend at least

£300 per annum; and there were other children. Still it is wrong to say, that it had become insufficient; as usual it had not come to that; but, on the first symptoms arising that it would soon come to that, somebody, of course, had notice to consider himself a sort of nuisance elect,—and in this case it was the Distributor of Stamps for the county of Cumberland." And in this strain of good-humoured banter—stimulated no doubt by his own precarious circumstances, in a measure, circumstances which ought not in his case to be precarious,—De Quincy relates how another £400 a year was added to the poet's income from the increase of his district as Stamp-Distributor.

In 1842, since De Quincy wrote the above, Wordsworth resigned this office, and it was bestowed upon his son,—whilst he (the poet,) was put down upon the Civil-list for £300 a year, and finally made Poet Laureate.

To return, however, to the more even tenor of these Memoirs:—A circumstance occurred in the year 1803, shortly after the Scottish tour, which will further illustrate the "good luck" of Wordsworth, although in this instance he did not avail himself of it. Sir George Beaumont, the painter, out of pure sympathy with the poet,—and before he had seen or written to him,—purchased a beautiful little estate at Applethwaite, near Keswick, and presented it to him, in order that he (Wordsworth) and Coleridge, who was then residing at Greta Hall, might have the pleasure of a nearer and more permanent intercourse. A fragment of Sir George's letter (good Sir George, who *could* recognise genius, and was noble and generous enough to prove his recognition in a most practical form) is printed in Dr. Wordsworth's " Memoirs," and it shews what a fine heart he had, God bless him! It is dated October 24, 1803, and runs thus :—

" I had a most ardent desire to bring you and Coleridge together. I thought with pleasure on the increase of enjoyment you would receive from the beauties of Nature, by being able to communicate more frequently your sensations to each other, and that this would be the means of contributing to the pleasure and improvement of the world, by stimulating you both to poetic exertions." The benevolent project of this excellent baronet was defeated, partly because Coleridge soon after left Greta Hall for a warmer climate, being impelled to this course by ill health, and partly from private considerations respecting Wordsworth and his family, which, however, do not transpire in the " Memoirs." A curious fact in connection with this gift of Sir George is, that Wordsworth neglected to thank the donor, or to take the slightest notice of it, for eight weeks after the writings were placed in his hands. In a letter addressed to the baronet, dated Grasmere, October 14th, 1803, Wordsworth apologises for this apparent neglect, and attributes it partly to the overpowering feelings with which the gift inspired him, and partly to a nervous dread of writing, and a fear lest he should acknowledge the honour that had been done him in an unworthy manner. " This feeling," he says, " was indeed so very strong in me, as to make me look upon the act of writing to you, not as the work of a moment, but as a thing not to be done, but in my best, my purest, my happiest moments." Thus strangely began one of the few friendships which Wordsworth cultivated with men, and one which lasted through the life of the noble-hearted baronet, who, in dying, in the year 1827 (on the 7th of February), left Wordsworth an annuity of £100 to defray the expenses of an annual tour. (Another instance of the poet's "good luck!") It is right to add, that Wordsworth was deeply affected by his friend's death, and that he has left, in his "Elegiac Musings," some noble lines to his memory.

Amongst the occasional visitors at Grasmere between the years 1800 and 1804, was Captain John Wordsworth, the poet's second brother, who was eventually lost in the Abergaveny East Indiaman, on the 5th of February, 1804. His brother was a man of fine taste and discernment, and prophesied in various letters and at various times, the ultimate success of Wordsworth's poetry. Wordsworth felt severely the untimely death of his brother, whom he loved with that devoted family fondness, which was characteristic of him. Writing to Sir George Beaumont upon this event, he says: "February 11th, 1808. This calamitous news we received at two o'clock to-day; and I write to you from a house of mourning. My poor sister, and my wife, who loved him almost as we did (for he was one of the most amiable of men) are in miserable affliction, which I do all in my power to alleviate; but, Heaven knows, I want consolation myself. I can say nothing higher of my ever dear brother than that he was worthy of his sister, who is now weeping beside me, and of the friendship of Coleridge; meek, affectionate, silently enthusiastic, loving all quiet things, and a poet in everything but words." The lyre of the poet sounded his praises in three poems. The first is entitled "Elegiac Stanzas suggested by a picture of Peel Castle in a storm, painted by Sir George Beaumont." The next is "To a Daisy," which suggests his brother's love of quiet and peaceful things, and closes with the tragedy of his death, and the discovery and final burial of the body in the country churchyard of Wythe, a village near Weymouth.

" And thou, sweet flower, shalt sleep and wake,
    Upon his senseless grave,' "

he concludes, returning thus finely to the simple flower which suggested the melancholy train of thought that runs through the poem. The third of these sad lyrical verses refers to the scene where the poet bade his brother farewell, on the mountains from Grasmere to Patterdale. The verses upon the "Picture of Peel Castle," is the best of all these pieces; and as a fitting conclusion to this brief memorial of the poet's brother, I will transcribe it.

"I was thy neighbour once, thou rugged pile!
    Four summer weeks I dwelt in sight of thee:
I saw thee every day; and all the while
    Thy form was sleeping on a glassy sea.

So pure thy sky, so quiet was the air!
    So like, so very like, was day to day!
Where'er I looked, thy image still was there;
    It trembled, but it never passed away.

How perfect was the calm! it seemed no sleep;
    No mood, which season takes away or brings:
I could have fancied that the mighty deep
    Was even the gentlest of all gentle things.

Ah! *then*, if mine had been the painter's hand,
    To express what then I saw; and add the gleam,
The light that never was on sea, or land,
    The consecration, and the poet's dream;

I would have planted thee, thou hoary pile!
    Amid a world how different from this!
Beside a sea that could not cease to smile
    On tranquil land, beneath a sky of bliss.

A picture had it been of lasting ease,
    Elysian quiet, without toil or strife;
No motion but the moving tide, a breeze,
    Or merely silent Nature's breathing life.

Such, in the fond illusion of my heart,
    Such picture would I at that time have made;
And seen the soul of truth in every part,
    A steadfast peace that might not be betrayed.

So once it would have been—'tis so no more;
    I have submitted to a new control;
A power is gone, which nothing can restore;
    A deep distress hath humanised my soul.

Not for a moment could I now behold
    A smiling sea, and be what I have been;
The feeling of my loss will ne'er be old;
    This, which I know, I speak with mind serene.

Then, Beaumont, friend! who would have been the friend,
    If he had lived, of him whom I deplore,
This work of thine I blame not, but commend;
    This sea in anger, and that dismal shore.

O 'tis a passionate work!—yet wise and well;
    Well chosen is the spirit that is here;
That hulk, which labours in the deadly swell,
    This rueful sky, this pageantry of fear!

And this huge castle, standing here sublime,
  I love to see the look with which it braves,
Cased in the unfeeling armour of old time,
  The lightning, the fierce wind, and trampling waves.

Farewell, farewell, the heart that lives alone,
  Housed in a dream, at distance from the kind!
Such happiness, wherever it be known,
  Is to be pitied, for 'tis surely blind.

But welcome fortitude, and patient cheer,
  And frequent sights of what is to be borne!
Such sights, or worse, as are before me here.—
  Not without hope we suffer, and we mourn."
                              —1805.

About a month after his brother's death, Wordsworth concluded his "Prelude," upon which he had been employed for upwards of six years. In allusion to this poem, Coleridge, in the "Table Talk," says: "I cannot help regretting that Wordsworth did not first publish his thirteen books (there are fourteen of them,) "On the growth of an individual mind,"—superior, as I used to think, on the whole, to the "Excursion!" . . . . Then the plan laid out, and I believe partly suggested by me was, that Wordsworth should assume the station of a man in mental repose, one whose principles were made up, and so prepared to deliver upon authority a system of philosophy. He was to treat man as man, a subject of eye, ear, touch and taste, in contact with external nature, and inferring the senses from the mind, and not compounding a mind out of the senses; then he was to describe the pastoral and other states of society, assuming something of the Juvenalian spirit as he approached the high civilization of cities and towns, and opening a melancholy picture of the present state of degeneracy and vice; thence he was to infer and reveal the proof of, and necessity for, the whole state of man and society being subject to, and illustrative of, a redemptive process in operation, showing how this idea reconciled all the anomalies, and promised future glory and restoration."

Wordsworth himself unfolds his own plan of the poem to Sir George Beaumont, in a letter dated December 25th, 1804. It was to consist, first of all, of a poem to be called "The Recluse," wherein the poet was to express in verse, his own feelings concerning Man, Nature, and Society—and, secondly, a poem on his *earlier life* or the *growth of his own mind.* This latter poem was "The Prelude," two thousand verses of which, he says, in the same letter, he had written during the last ten weeks. "The Prelude," therefore, which was not published till after the poet's death, was first written, and "The Recluse," subsequently. Only a part of this poem, however—viz., "The Excursion," except, of course, "The Prelude," is published; "The Recluse" Proper, being still in MS.

Besides these larger works, Wordsworth threw off—not without care and meditation,—for no man ever wrote with more method and purpose—many minor poems, and amongst them was "The Waggoner," dedicated to Charles Lamb, but not published until 1819. It was in this year (1805) that Wordsworth, Sir Walter Scott, and Sir Humphry Davy ascended Helvellyn together; and learned the sad story of poor Charles Gough, who perished in attempting to cross over Helvellyn to Grasmere, by slipping from a steep part of the rock, where the ice was not thawed, and beside whose remains his faithful dog was found many days afterwards, almost starved to death. This affecting incident afforded a theme for both poets—viz., Sir Walter and Wordsworth, and each wrote upon it without knowing that the other was similarly engaged. Scott's poem is entitled "Helvellyn," and Wordsworth's "Fidelity."

In 1807, Wordsworth issued two new volumes of poetry, in 12mo., which contained some of his best pieces; but which, like all his poems, did not gain immediate popularity. It is true that a fourth edition of the "Lyrical Ballads" had been called for, and that this indicated a growing taste in the public mind for Wordsworth's effusions; but the critics assailed him with the bitterest animosity, and on the whole without much reason. With no reason, in short, so far as the poetic principles —the canon of his poetry—was concerned, and only with some show of reason in the instance of his peculiar mannerism. For although he was often misled by his craving after simplicity, and uttered what might be called without any violation of truth or desecration of the poet's name and memory—*drivel*—still he had published poems of a very high order, such as had not been published in the lifetime of any man then living. The critics, however, could not let him alone, could not see the manifest beauties of his poetry, or *would* not see them, but denounced the whole without reserve or mercy. In the meanwhile Coleridge cheered him on, and on his return to England, in the summer of 1806, Wordsworth read "The Prelude" to him in the gardens of Coleorton, near Ashby-de-la-Zouch, Leicestershire, where the poet was then residing at the invitation of Sir George Beaumont; and the high commendations which Coleridge poured upon this poem animated Wordsworth to increased exertion and perseverance. During his residence at this beautiful house, he composed the noble "Song at the Feast of Brougham Castle,"— the finest thing of the kind in our language; and he left behind him as usual, many records of his feelings at Coleorton. The poet's letters to Sir George Beaumont and an occasional one to Sir Walter Scott, are amongst the most interesting transcripts we have of his mind at this period.

It was in the beginning of the winter, 1807, that De Quincy paid his first visit to Wordsworth; and I find great fault with Dr.

Wordsworth that he makes no allusion to De Quincy in all his memoirs of the poet. This is the more unpardonable, inasmuch as De Quincy is a man of the highest calibre—of the most refined taste,—of the profoundest scholarship, and possessing the widest acquaintance with general literature—to say nothing of his transcendant genius—of any man who has lived in this generation. Unpardonable, likewise, because De Quincy was a devout lover, and a chivalrous defender of Wordsworth, when it was not fashionable to speak well of him, and when a man who praised him stood a fair chance of being estimated, if not called, a madman. Neither can I ever forgive the poet himself for his cold neglect of the great Opium Eater. Such a man as De Quincy is not to be treated with contumely and despite, even by such a man as Wordsworth; for assuredly, in point of genius, both men stood pretty much upon the same level, and Wordsworth was far inferior to De Quincy in the other important matters specified above. De Quincy's demon did not inspire him to write verses, but to write essays—and what essays! I do not know the writer who has ever taken so wide a range of subjects, and written upon them in such grand and noble English. De Quincy was a prose architect, Wordsworth a poetic one; and this is all the difference between them. In genius they were equal. Some day, perhaps, De Quincy will be better appreciated. We are indebted to De Quincy for the best account existing of the poet, his family, and home at Grasmere and Rydal; and no one would go to Dr. Wordsworth for information when he could go to De Quincy. Not that I have anything to say against Dr. Wordsworth personally, but I dislike his studied exclusiveness. The men who for long years were in constant intercourse with the poet, and on terms of friendship with him—Wilson, for example, as well as De Quincy—cannot be shut out from his biography without manifest injustice both to them and to the poet; and yet this is systematically done. Perhaps the good doctor has a clerical horror of his great-uncle being associated with loose Men of Letters; men, too, of not quite an orthodox cast in their opinions; genial, jovial, and full of all good fellowship besides. But of what avail could such horror so manifested be? The world *will* know the truth at last; and it is right they should; and one thing is certain enough, that Wordsworth will suffer no dishonour in the companionship of De Quincy and Wilson.

When I first read No. 1, of the "Lake Reminiscences," by De Quincy, in "Tait's Magazine," I could scarcely believe what I read; and nothing would have convinced me of its truth, short of the authority which announced it. I had looked upon Wordsworth as a kind-hearted, generous, and unselfish man; noble, friendly, and without the vanity which has so often blurred the fair page of a great man's nature. I was sorry to find that I was mistaken in this estimate of the poet; and that he, like me, and all the rest of us, had faults and failings manifold. De Quincy's own account of his first visit to Wordsworth, the deep reverence with which he regarded him, and the overwhelming feelings which beset him on the occasion, is very affecting; and contrasted with the poet's subsequent treatment of him, his wanton throwing away of that noble and affectionate heart, and his total disregard of the high intellectual homage which De Quincy offered to him, is still more affecting, and full, likewise, of pain and sorrow. Whilst he was a student at Oxford, De Quincy twice visited the Lake Country, on purpose to pay his respects to Wordsworth; and once, he says, he went forward from Coniston to the very gorge of Hammerscar, " from which the whole vale of Grasmere suddenly breaks upon the view in a style of almost theatrical surprise, with its lovely valley stretching in the distance, the lake lying immediately below, with its solemn boat-like island, of five acres in size, seemingly floating on its surface; its exquisite outline on the opposite shore, revealing all its little bays, and wild sylvan margin, feathered to the edge with wild flowers and ferns!

"In one quarter a little wood, stretching for about half a mile towards the outlet of the lake, more directly in opposition to the spectator; a few green fields: and beyond them, just two bow-shots from the water, a little white cottage gleaming from the midst of trees, with a vast and seemingly never-ending series of ascents, rising above it to the height of more than three thousand feet. That little cottage was Wordsworth's, from the time of his marriage, until 1808. Afterwards, for many a year, it was mine. Catching one glimpse of this loveliest of landscapes, I retreated, like a guilty thing, for fear I might be surprised by Wordsworth, and then returned faint-hearted to Coniston, and so to Oxford, *re infecta.*— This was in 1806. And thus, from mere excess of nervous distrust in my own powers for sustaining a conversation with Wordsworth, I had for nearly five years shrunk from a meeting for which, beyond all things under heaven, I longed."

This nervous distrust yielded in after life to a sober confidence, and a matchless power of unfolding his thoughts colloquially. In the meanwhile, that is to say, in 1807, Coleridge returned from Malta, and De Quincy was introduced to him first of all at Bridgewater, and met him again at the Hot-wells, near Bristol, —when, upon discovering that he was anxious to put his wife and children under some friendly escort, on their return homewards to Keswick, De Quincy offered to unite with Mrs. Coleridge in a post-chaise to the north. Accordingly they set out. Hartley Coleridge was then nine years old, Derwent about seven, and the beautiful little daughter about five. In such companionship, then, did De Quincy pay his first visit to Wordsworth, at Grasmere,—a most interesting and artistic account of which he has written in "Tait's Magazine," and to which I have been frequently indebted in the compilation of these Memoirs. The cottage has already been described, and the reader who has followed the course of this imperfect history, will remember the portraits of its illustrious inmates. Let us now see how it fared with De Quincy, when he met the mighty man of his heart. He was "stunned," when Wordsworth shook him cordially by the hand, and went mechanically towards the house, leaving Mrs. Coleridge in the chaise at the door. The re-appearance of the poet, however, after exercising due hospitality to his lady guest, gave him courage, and he found that the said poet was, after all, but a man. His reverence for him, however, continued unabated, and for twenty-five years, during which time De Quincy lived at the lakes, in constant communion with Wordsworth, his reverence for the poet's genius remained the same, and still remains, although he has long since ceased to respect him so highly as a man; not, however, because Wordsworth was not of unimpeachable character, and estimable in so many ways, but because he had not that generous love for his friends which friendship demands. De Quincy confesses his estrangement from the poet with sorrow, and some bitterness of heart; and the following extract will throw all the light upon this subject which can be thrown at present:—

"I imagine a case such as this which follows," says De Quincy, in alluding to the estrangement spoken of above—"the case of a man who for many years has connected himself with the domestic griefs and joys of another, over and above his primary service of giving to him the strength and the encouragement of a profound literary sympathy, at a time of universal scorning from the world; suppose this man to fall into a situation, in which, from want of natural connections, and from his state of insulation in life, it might be most important to his feelings that some support should be lent to him by a friend having a known place and acceptation, and what may be called a root in the country, by means of connections, descent, and long settlement. To look for this might be a most humble demand on the part of one who had testified his devotion in the way supposed. To miss it might——But enough. I murmur not; complaint is weak at all times; and the hour is passed irrevocably, and by many a year, in which an act of friendship so natural, and costing so little (in both senses so priceless), could have been availing. The ear is deaf that should have been solaced by the sound of welcome. Call, but you will not be heard; shout aloud, but your 'ave!' and 'all hail!' will now tell only as an echo of departed days, proclaiming the hollowness of human hopes. I, for my part, have long learned the lesson of suffering in silence; and also I have learned to know that, wheresoever female prejudices are concerned, *there* it will be a trial, more than Herculean, of a man's wisdom, if he can walk with an even step, and swerve neither to the right nor to the left."

Leaving this sad subject, however, let us return to De Quincy at Grasmere in 1807. Mrs. Coleridge, on leaving the poet's family for Keswick, invited De Quincy to visit her and Southey, and it was arranged that Wordsworth and the Opium Eater should go together.

Accordingly they set off in a farmer's cart to Ambleside, and from thence mounted the ascent of Kirkstone. Descending towards Brothers' Water—" a lake which lies immediately below; and about three miles further, through endless woods, and under the shade of mighty fells, immediate dependencies and processes of the still more mighty Helvellyn" they approached the vale of Patterdale, and reached the inn, by moonlight. "All I remember," says De Quincy is—" that through those romantic woods and rocks of Stybarren—through those silent glens of Glencoin and Glenridding—through that most romantic of parks then belonging to the Duke of Norfolk—viz., Gobarrow Park—we saw alternately for four miles, the most grotesque and the most awful spectacles—

———" Abbey windows
And Moorish temples of the Hindoos,"

all fantastic, all as unreal and shadowy as the moon-light which created them; whilst at every angle of the road, broad gleams came upwards of Ullswater, stretching for nine miles northward, but fortunately for its effect, broken into three watery channels of about equal length, and rarely visible at once."

The party, (for Miss Wordsworth and the poet's children were present on this occasion,) passed the night in a house called *Ewsmere*, and in the morning, leaving his family at this inn, the poet set out, with De Quincy, for a ramble through the woods of Lowther. These are the woods concerning which the poet, in a letter to Sir George Beaumont, dated October 17, 1805, says :—" I believe a more delightful spot is not under the sun. Last summer I had a charming walk along the river, for which I was indebted to this man [alluding to a good quaker, who was Lord Lowther's *arbiter elegantiarum*, or master of the grounds, and who was making improvements in them, by virtue of his office], whose intention is to carry the walk along the river side till it joins the great road at Lowther Bridge, which you will recollect, just under Brougham, about a mile from Penrith.. This, to my great sorrow! for the manufactured walk, which was absolutely necessary in many places, will, in one place, pass through a few hundred yards of forest-ground, and will there efface the most beautiful specimen of forest pathway ever seen by human eyes, and which I have paced many an hour when I was a youth, with one of those I best loved. There is a continued opening between the trees, a narrow slip of green turf, besprinkled with flowers, chiefly daisies; and here it is that this pretty path plays its pranks, weaving among the turf and flowers at its pleasure." And it was in these woods, just five days after their introduction to each other, that Wordsworth and De Quincy spent a whole glorious morning in wild ramblings and in conversation. They dined together, towards evening, at Emont Bridge, and then walked on to the house of Captain Wordsworth, at Penrith. The family was absent, and the poet had business which occupied him all the next day; so De Quincy took a walk, sauntering along the road, about seventeen miles, to Keswick, where he enquired for Greta Hall, the residence of the poet Southey. " It stands out of the town a few hundred yards, upon a little eminence, overhanging the river Greta." Mrs. Coleridge and Southey came to the door to welcome their visitor. " Southey was in person somewhat taller than Wordsworth, being about five feet eleven in height, or a trifle more, whilst Wordsworth was about five feet ten; and partly from having slenderer limbs, partly from being more symmetrically formed about the shoulders, than Wordsworth, he struck me as a better and lighter figure, to the effect of which his dress contributed; for he wore, pretty constantly, a short jacket and pantaloons, and had much the air of a Tyrolese mountaineer. . . . His hair was black, and yet his complexion was fair; his eyes, I believe, hazel, and large, but I will not vouch for that fact; his nose aquiline; and he had a remarkable habit of looking up into the air, as if looking at abstraction. The expression of his face was that of a very acute, and an aspiring man. So far it was even noble, as it conveyed a feeling of serene and gentle pride, habitually familiar with elevating subjects of contemplation. And yet it was impossible that this pride could have been offensive to anybody, chastened as it was by the most unaffected modesty; and this modesty made evident and prominent, by the constant expression of reverence for the great men of the age (when he happened to esteem them such), and for all the great patriarchs of our literature. The point in which

Southey, however, failed most in conciliating regard was, in all which related to the external expression of friendliness. No man could be more sincerely hospitable, no man more completely disposed to give up, even his time (the possession which he most valued), to the service of his friends; but, there was an air of reserve and distance about him—the reserve of a lofty, self-respecting mind, but, perhaps, a little too freezing,—in his treatment of all persons who were not amongst the *corps* of his ancient fireside friends. Still, even towards the veriest strangers, it is but justice to notice his extreme courtesy, in sacrificing his literary employments for the day, whatever they might be, to the duty (for such he made it,) of doing the honors of the lake, and the adjacent mountains."

De Quincy says that the habits of the poet Southey were exceedingly regular, and that all his literary business was conducted upon a systematic plan. He had his task before breakfast, which, however, must have been an inconsiderable nothing, for it occupied him only an hour, and rarely that, for he never rose until eight, and always breakfasted at nine o'clock. He went to bed precisely at half-past ten, and no sleep short of nine hours, refreshed him, and enabled him to do his work. He usually dined between five and six, and his chief labour was done between breakfast and dinner. If he had visitors, he would sit over his wine, and talk; if not, he retired to his library, until eight, when he was summoned to tea. At ten he read the London papers; " and it was perfectly astonishing," says De Quincy, " to men of less methodical habits, to find how much he got through of elaborate business, by his unvarying system of arrangement in the distribution of his time." All his letters were answered on the same day that they arrived. Even his poetry was written by forced efforts, or rather, perhaps, by what De Quincy calls, " a predetermined rule." It was by writing prose, however, that Southey got his living—made " his pot boil," as he says; and his chief source of regular income was derived from " The Quarterly Review." At one time, however, he received £400 a year for writing the historical part of " The Edinburgh Annual Register." This, however, he gave up, because the publisher proposed to dock £100 from the salary which he had previously paid him.—

Southey, however, could afford to lose this large income, because he had an annuity which had been settled upon him by his friend, Charles Wynne, "the brother of Sir Watkin, the great autocrat of Wales." This annuity, however, when his friend married, Southey voluntarily gave up; and the Granvilles, to whom Wynne was related by his marriage, placed Southey on the civil list, for the sacrifice which he thus made.

Such, then, were the circumstances of Southey at the time of De Quincy's visit, and it must be owned that they were very comfortable, for a poet. Wordsworth came on the day after De Quincy's arrival, and it was evident that the two poets were not on the most friendly terms; not that there was any outward sign of this,—on the contrary, there were all the exteriors of hospitality and good feeling on both sides; but De Quincy saw that the spiritual link between them was not complete, but broken; that, indeed, they did not understand, or fully sympathise with each other. Their minds and habits were different—I had almost said totally different. Wordsworth lived on the mountain top, composed there, and drew his inspiration direct from Nature; Southey lived in his magnificent library, and was inspired more by books than by natural objects.— Wordsworth's library consisted of two or three hundred volumes, mostly torn and dilapidated; many were odd volumes; they were ill bound— not bound—or put in boards. Leaves were often wanting, and their place supplied occasionally by manuscript. These books "occupied a little homely book-case, fixed into one of two hollow recesses, formed on each side of the fireplace by the projection of the chimney into the little solitary room up stairs, which he had already described as his 'half kitchen, half parlour.' . . . . Southey's collection occupied a separate room—the largest, and every way the most agreeable in the house."

Wordsworth's poetry was *subjective*—referred chiefly to the inner life of man; and his dealings with Nature had a special reference to this inner life, his imagery being the mere vehicle of his thought. Southey's poetry, on the contrary, was essentially *objective*,—a reflex of the outward nature, heightened by the fiery colouring of his imagination. Wordsworth had a contempt for books, or, at all events, for *most* books,—whilst Southey's library, as De Quincy says, was his estate. Wordsworth would toss books about like tennis balls; and to let him into your library, quoth Southey, " is like letting a bear into a tulip-garden." De Quincy relates, that Wordsworth being one morning at breakfast with him at Grasmere, took a handsome volume of Burke's from his book-case, and began very leisurely to cut the leaves with a knife smeared all over with butter. Now tastes and habits such as those which marked the two poets could not unite them very closely together; at all events, not at this time; although they were subsequently, and in later years, upon terms of close intimacy and friendship. Upon the present occasion, however,—that is to say, during De Quincy's visit to Southey—the two poets managed very well together, and the evening was passed agreeably enough. Next morning they discussed politics, and to the horror of De Quincy, who was then a young man, and took no interest in the passing movements of nations, and had always heard the French Revolution, and its barbaric excesses, stigmatised as infernal,—who was, moreover a loyal person according to the tradition of his fathers, and a lover of Mr. Pitt—to his horror, the two poets uttered the most disloyal sentiments, denouncing all monarchial forms of government, and proposed to send the royal family to Botany Bay! This proposal, which Southey immediately threw into extempore verse, was so comical, that the whole party laughed outright, and outrageously; they then set off towards Grasmere.

De Quincy speaks in the highest terms of Southey, and in the comparison which he institutes between Southey and Wordsworth, the latter certainly sustains loss. I refer the reader to the "Lake Reminiscences" for this, and other most interesting particulars relating to these poets. Still I cannot bid adieu to these "Reminiscences," without using them once more, as materials for an account of Greta Hall and its occupants.

Southey and his family did not occupy the whole of the Hall, but shared it with Coleridge and his family, and with Mrs. Lovell and her son. There was no absolute partition, but an amicable distribution of the rooms. Coleridge had a study to himself, in which was a grand organ, about the only piece of furniture it could boast of. To atone for this, the windows looked out upon a magnificent sweep of country, and objects of sublimity and beauty met the eye wherever it wandered. Southey's library—already described as the best room of the house—was open to all the ladies alike. The books in it were chiefly " English, Spanish, and Portuguese, well selected, being the best cardinal classics of the three literatures; fine copies, and decorated externally with a reasonable elegance, so as to make them in harmony with the other embellishments of the room. This was aided by the horizontal arrangement, upon brackets, of many rare manuscripts, Spanish or Portuguese. The two families always met at dinner, in a common drawing-room.

The scenery around Greta Hall was grand beyond all power of description. " The lake of Derwent Water, in one direction, with its lovely islands—a lake about ten miles in circuit, and shaped pretty much like a boy's kite; the lake of Bassinthwaite in another; the mountains of Newlands, arranging themselves like pavilions; the gorgeous confusion of Borrowdale, just revealing its sublime chaos through the narrow vista of its gorge; whilst the sullen rear, not fully visible on this side of the house, was closed for many a league by the vast and towering masses of Skiddaw and Blencathara—mountains which are rather to be considered as frontier barriers, and chains of hilly ground, cutting the county of Cumberland into great chambers, and different climates, than as insulated eminences; so vast is the area which they occupy; though there are, also, rich, separate, and insulated heights, and nearly amongst the highest in the county."

Such, then, is the description of Southey's house and neighbourhood, as given by De Quincy. The first visit of the Opium Eater to Wordsworth—including these visits to Greta Hall, and wanderings through the lake districts —extended over a week; and at the conclusion of that time, when it was necessary for him to return to Oxford, to save his Michaelmas term, he witnessed, and has described one of the most extraordinary scenes, at the table of the woman with the "*Saracen's Head,*" in company with Wordsworth and his sister, that has, perhaps, ever been enacted at any supper table in the kingdoms of this world. I can give no account of it here, and refer the reader once more to the " Reminiscences:" all I will say, in conclusion is, that in the following November (1808), De Quincy returned to Grasmere, and took possession of the late cottage of the poet; who, with his family, had removed to a house, called Allan Bank, about three-quarters of a mile off, which had recently been built by a Liverpool merchant, at a cost of £1,500; a damp, cold, and incurably smoky house, which defects the poet set forth so eloquently to the proprietor, that he allowed him to live in it for a merely nominal rent.

The reason for Wordsworth's removal, was the increasing number of his family. And here I may as well give a list of this family, adding to it the only one who was born after the period to which I now allude. They are as follow:—

John, born 18th June, 1803.

Dorothy, called, and generally known as, Dora, born 16th August, 1804.

Thomas, born 16th June, 1806.

Catharine, born 6th September, 1808.

William, born 12th May, 1810.

Thomas and Catharine, died in their childhood; John and William are still living; and Dora, " My own Dora," as the poet loved to call her, after a wedded life, more or less happy (she married Edward Quillinan, Esq.), she died in 1847, just three years before her venerable father.

Wordsworth was singularly fortunate in his family. There was no jars nor discords in the sacred temple of his home; but beauty, love, and all the virtues and the graces dwelt with him, and ministered to his happiness and repose. He loved his children with an intense affection; and sweet Dora, his best beloved, exercised an influence over him, more beautiful and harmonising perhaps, even than that which his sister exercised in his early life, and still continued to exercise, because it was deeper, and struck deeper into the very being of the poet. This child threw a sacred halo round his soul, and inspired one of the sweetest of his lyrics. Only a month after her birth he wrote :—

" Hast thou then survived
Mild offspring of infirm humanity ?
. . . . Hail to thee !
Frail, feeble monthling. . . On thy face

Smiles are beginning, like the beams of dawn,
To shoot, and circulate. Smiles have there been seen;
Tranquil assurances that heaven supports
The feeble motions of thy life, and cheers
Thy loveliness; or shall those smiles be called
Feelers of love, put forth as if to explore
This untried world, and to prepare thy way
Through a strait passage intricate and dim?"

In the autumn of the same year we find him writing the lines "The Kitten and the Falling Leaves," suggested by the delight of his dear Dora at the pretty frolics of a kitten on the wall, playing with the leaves of autumn.

"Such a light of gladness breaks
 Pretty kitten! from thy freaks;
 Spreads with such a living grace,
 O'er my little Dora's face."

then the poet resolves that he will have his glee out of life:—

" I will have my careless season,
  Spite of melancholy reason;
  Will walk thro' life in such a way,
  That, when time brings on decay,
  Now and then, I may possess
  Hours of perfect gladsomeness;

>   Keep the sprightly soul awake,
>   And have faculties to take,
>   Even from things by sorrow wrought,
>   Matter for a jocund thought;
>   Spite of care and spite of grief,
>   To gambol with life's falling leaf."

He likewise addresses "The Longest Day" to her; and what a contrast to the last poem! Instead of gambolling with the falling leaves, and making life a grand holiday, he exhorts his child, now grown older, to think of higher matters :—

> " Summer ebbs; each day that follows
>   Is a reflex from on high,
> Tending to the darksome hollows,
>   Where the frosts of winter lie.
> Now, even now, e'er wrapped in slumber,
>   Fix thine eyes upon the sea,
> That absorbs time, space, and number,—
>   Look thou to eternity !"

And a little later, when the possibility of blindness came like a gloomy shadow to darken his more thoughtful moments; he anticipates the time when his own Dora shall guide his lonely steps. Poor Dora! she died of consumption, after trying, in vain, the warm south of Portugal. And yet she is not dead, and cannot die. In Dr. Wordsworth's Memoirs, second volume, there is a fine portrait of her, and a sweet, mild, gentle, and spiritual girl she is; the eye singularly beautiful, and full of deep mystic fire. The poet has also drawn a portrait of her :—

> " Open, ye thickets! let her fly,
> Swift as a Thracian nymph, o'er field or height!
> For she, to all but those who love her, shy,
> Would gladly vanish from a stranger's sight;
> Tho' where she is beloved, and loves
> Light as the wheeling butterfly she moves;
> Her happy spirit as a bird is free,
> That rifles blossoms on a tree,
> Turning them inside out, with rich audacity."

And all this sweet surfeit of painting is true to the spirit of the beautiful girl; the spirit which stirs her thoughts, and makes all her movements an impulsive comminglement of music and poetry. A more airy, celestial form could not be imagined than hers. It seems to float on the atmosphere. And then she is so happy, and loving to those who love her.

> " Alas! how little can a moment show
> Of an eye where feeling plays

In ten thousand dewy rays;
A face o'er which a thousand shadows go!—
She stops—is fastened to that rivulet's side;
And these (while, with sedater mien
O'er timid waters that have scarcely left
Their birthplace in the rocky cleft,
She bends) at leisure may be seen
Features to old ideal grace allied,
Amid their smiles and dimples dignified—
Fit countenance for the soul of primal truth;
The bland composure of eternal youth!

What more changeful than the sea?
But over his great tides
Fidelity presides;
And this light-hearted maiden constant is as he.
High is her aim, as heaven above,
And wide as ether her good will;
And like the lowly reed, her love
Can drink its nurture from the scantiest rill;
Insight as keen as frosty star
Is to her charity no bar,
Nor interrupts her frolic graces
When she is far from those wild places,
Encircled by familiar faces.

O the charms that manners draw,
Nature, from thy genuine law!
If from what her hand would do
Her voice would utter, aught ensue
  Untoward or unfit;

> She in benign affections pure
> In self-forgetfulness, secure,
> Sheds round the transient harm, or vague mischance
> A light unknown to tutored elegance:
> Hers is not a cheek shame-stricken,
> But her blushes, are joy-flushes;
> And the fault, if fault it be,
> Only ministers to quicken
> Laughter-loving gaiety,
> And kindly sportive wit,
> Leaving this daughter of the mountains free
> As if she knew that Oberon, king of faery
> Had crossed her purpose with some quaint vagary,
> And heard his viewless bands
> Over their mirthful triumph clapping hands."

A fairer drawn portrait—a more beautiful poem, as a whole—does not, I think, exist. Alas! sweet Dora.

To return, however, to the narrative. When Wordsworth was living at Allan Bank, and during the time that Coleridge sojourned with him, two prose works appeared, by these two poets, which are memorable to all scholars. The former wrote his famous "Essay on the Convention of Cintra," and the latter dictated (for he did not write it) his still more famous work entitled "The Friend." Notwithstanding Wordsworth's devotion, therefore, to poetry, it will be seen that he was not indifferent to the passing events which were writing their history in the blood of nations. Speaking of his " Convention of Cintra," in a letter to Southey, he says, " My detestation, I may say abhorrence, of that event, is not at all diminished by your account of it. Bonaparte had committed a capital blunder in supposing that when he had *intimidated* the *Sovereigns* of Europe, he had *conquered* the several nations. Yet it was natural for a wiser than he was to have fallen into this mistake; for the old despotisms had deprived the body of the people of all practical knowledge in the management, and of necessity of all interest in the course of affairs. The French themselves were astonished at the apathy and ignorance of the people whom they had supposed they had utterly subdued, when they had taken their fortresses, scattered their armies, entered their capital cities, and struck their cabinets with dismay. There was no hope for the deliverance of Europe till the nations had suffered enough to be driven to a passionate recollection of all that was honourable in their past history, and to make appeal to the principles of universal and everlasting justice. These sentiments the authors of that Convention most unfeelingly violated; and as to the principals, they seemed to be as little aware even of the existence of such powers, for powers emphatically may they be called, as the tyrant himself. As far, therefore, as these men could, they put an extinguisher upon the star that was then rising ! It is in vain to say that after the first burst of indignation was over, the Portuguese themselves were reconciled to the event, and rejoiced in their deliverance. We may infer from that, the horror which they must have felt in the presence of their oppressors; and we may see in it to what a state of helplessness their bad government had reduced them. Our duty was to have treated them with respect, as the representatives of suffering humanity, beyond what they were likely to look for themselves, and as deserving greatly, in common with their Spanish brethren, for having been the first to rise against that tremendous oppression, and to show how, and how only, it could be put an end to." The poet apologises for the seeming inconsistency of his conduct in opposing the war against France at its commencement, and in urging the necessity of it in the later affairs of Spain and Portugal, by showing that he, and those who thought with him, " proved that they kept their eyes steadily fixed upon principles; for though there was a shifting or transfer of hostility in their minds, as far as regarded persons, they only combated the same enemy opposed to them under a different shape; and that enemy was the spirit of selfish tyranny and lawless ambition."

So far, then, the " Essay on the Convention of Cintra." Coleridge's prose work, " The Friend," was a serial, composed of papers upon various subjects, written mostly by Coleridge himself, with occasional assistance from Wordsworth, Professor Wilson, and others. In the seventeenth number of " The Friend," the latter writer, in a letter to the Editor, speaks of Wordsworth as a "great teacher," and a "mighty voice not poured out in vain." " There are hearts," he says, " that have received into their inmost depths all its varying tones; and even now there are many to whom the name of Wordsworth calls up the recollection of their weakness. and the consciousness of their strength." The letter was signed " Mathetes," and might be called a warning voice to the young upon the illusions and popular fallacies of the age. It insisted likewise upon the dues belonging to antiquity; combated the notion that human nature is gradually advancing to perfection, and that the present time is wiser than the past. "Mathetes" maintained that reliance on contemporary judgment had grown into contempt for antiquity, and argued that the youth of his time could only be rescued from this perilous condition by the warning voice of some contemporary teacher; and that this teacher he imagined Wordsworth to be.

Wordsworth replied, in numbers seventeen and twenty, acknowledging that we are too apt to value contemporary opinion, to the neglect of antiquity; but denying that the doctrine of progress is injurious; and exhorting the young to rely upon themselves, and their own independent efforts; cherishing along with this, an abiding sense of personal responsibility. I cannot, however, analyse the fine treatise which follows, and must refer the reader to the treatise itself; merely adding, that a sounder or more philosophical discourse—so practical withal—has rarely been written. An "Essay on

Epitaphs," was subsequently written by Wordsworth in "The Friend," February 22nd, 1810, and was afterwards republished by him, as a note to "The Excursion." Wordsworth regarded epitaphs as holy memorials, and censured the epigramatic efforts of Pope, and other writers of this species of composition. A bad man, he says, should have no epitaph; and that which the poet wrote over his own child, in the churchyard of Grasmere, may be instanced as illustrating his own idea of what epitaphs should be.

In the year 1810, Wordsworth wrote an introduction to, and edited the text of, a folio volume entitled, "Select Views in Cumberland, Westmoreland, and Lancashire;" by the Rev. Joseph Wilkinson, which were afterwards printed in his volume of "Sonnets on the River Duddon," and still later, as a separate publication. This introduction and text consisted of a description of the Lake Country, which is finer than anything of the kind existing, if we except the delicate and beautiful picture-writing of Gray, the poet, who visited this district in October 1767. And here end the chief incidents in the personal and literary life of Wordsworth, up to the time of his removal to Rydal Mount.

RYDAL MOUNT.

I must here borrow the only picture which I find in Dr. Wordsworth's " Memoirs,"—viz., that of the poet's residence, which I transcribe from vol. I., p. 19.

" The house stands on the sloping summit of a rocky hill, called Nab's Scar. It has a southern aspect. In front of it is a small semi-circular area of grey gravel, fringed with shrubs and flowers, the house forming the diameter of the circle. From this area is a descent of a few stone steps southward, and then a gentle ascent to a grassy mound. Here let us rest a little.— At your back is the house; in front, a little to the left of the horizon, is Wansfell, on which the light of the evening sun rests, and to which the poet has paid a grateful tribute in two of his sonnets :—

> 'Wansfell! this household has a favoured lot,
> Living with liberty on thee to gaze.'

Beneath it the blue smoke shews the place of the town of Ambleside. In front is the lake Windermere, shining in the sun; also in front, but more to the right, are the fells of Loughrigg, on which the poet's imagination pleased to plant a solitary castle:

> 'Ærial rock, whose solitary brow
> From this low threshold daily meets the sight.'

Looking to the right, in the garden, is a beautiful glade, overhung with rhododendrons, in beautiful leaf and bloom. Near them is a tall ash-tree, in which a thrush has sung for hours together, during many years. Not far from it is a laburnum, in which the osier cage of the doves was hung. Below, to the west, is the vegetable garden, not planted off from the rest, but blended with it by parterres of flowers and shrubs.

Returning to the platform of grey gravel

before the house, we pass under the shade of a fine sycamore, and ascend to the westward by fourteen steps of stones, about nine feet long, in the interstices of which grow the yellow flowering poppy, and the wild geranium, or Poor Robin,

'Gay
With his red stalks, upon a sunny day,'

a favourite with the poet, as his verses show.— The steps above, northward, lead to an upward *sloping terrace*, about two hundred and fifty feet long. On the right side it is shaded by laburnums, Portugal laurels, mountain-ash, and fine walnut-trees and cherries; on the left it is flanked by a low stone wall, coped with rude slates, and covered with lichens, mosses, and wild-flowers. The fern waves on the walls, and at its base grows the wild-strawberry and foxglove. Beneath this wall, and parallel to it, on the left, is a *level terrace*, constructed by the poet for a friend most dear to him and his,— who, for the last twenty years of Mr. Wordsworth's life, was often a visitor at Rydal Mount. The terrace was a favourite resort of the poet, being more easy for pacing to and fro, when old age began to make him feel the acclivity of the other terrace to be toilsome. Both these terraces command beautiful views of the vale of the Rothsay, and the banks of the lake of Windermere."

Then we have a description of Rydal Lake, and of the " long, wooded, and rocky hill of Loughrigg beyond, and above it," as seen from an orifice on the ascending terrace; of the beautiful sycamore close to the arbour, the fine firs in the foreground, and the dark woods of fir, ash, oak, hazel, holly, and birch, on the right and left; of the " FAR FERRDEL on the mountain's side," a little to the right of the " ascending terrace"—which, after a serpentine course of one hundred and fifty feet, terminates at a little gate, close to the " Nab Well," where the poet was wont to quaff his daily libations. Another walk from the arbour leads to a field, sloping down to the valley, called " Dora's field," and on the right is a rude stone, bearing this inscription—

> " In these fair vales hath many a tree
> At Wordsworth's suit been spared;
> And from the builder's hand this stone,
> For some rude beauty of its own,

>   Was rescued by the bard.
>   So let it rest, and time will come,
>   When here, the tender-hearted,
>   May heave a gentle sigh for him,
>   As one of the departed."

A pond containing gold fish, underneath a large oak, close to the gate which leads to this "Dora's field," completes the inventory of the external features of Rydal Mount.

It was in the spring of 1811 that Wordsworth left Allan Bank, and took up his temporary residence at the Parsonage, Grasmere. But the death of his children, Catharine and Thomas, which occurred in 1812, threw so melancholy a gloom over the neighbourhood, that he resolved to quit it altogether. It was not, however, without many painful feelings of regret that he bade adieu to the beautiful scenery in the vale of Grasmere—scenery which he had so long loved—every feature of which was as familiar to him as the faces of the dear children whom he had committed for ever to its quiet keeping. The step, however, was absolutely necessary, as he himself says in a letter to the Earl of Lonsdale, for the recurrence of that tranquillity of mind which it was his duty, and that of his surviving family, to strive for. Accordingly he removed to Rydal Mount, in 1813, where he resided until his death, in 1850. It was in that year—1813—that he received the appointment of Distributor of Stamps in the County of Westmoreland, which has already been alluded to, in the extracts made from the " Reminiscences" of De Quincy.

This appointment, for which he was mainly indebted to Lord Lonsdale, placed the poet in easy if not affluent circumstances, and enabled him to follow his art without anxiety respecting worldly matters,—a condition which the poet improved to his own honour, and to the public advantage. Some time after this good fortune had befallen him, he was offered the collectorship of the town of Whitehaven, an office far more lucrative than the other; but the poet declined it. He had now sufficient for his necessities, and no pecuniary inducement could avail with him to quit the sweet retirement of the lakes. He was fortunate, also—and De Quincy was right in saying that he was *always* fortunate, for Good Luck " threw her old shoe after him" wherever he went—in securing about this time the services of Mr. John Carter, as coadjutor in the stamp-office. Dr. Wordsworth speaks in the highest terms of this gentleman, who, for thirty-seven years, served the poet " faithfully and zealously, and who added to his business qualifications, those of sound scholarship and judicious criticism.

Thus happily circumstanced, Wordsworth continued to write poetry, and to make more tours, as his fancy dictated. In 1814, he again visited Scotland, in company with his wife, his wife's sister, and Miss Mary Hutchinson. The poems produced on this tour were " The Brownie's Cell," " Cora Linn," " Effusions on the Banks of the Bran, near Dunkeld," and " Sonnet to Mr. Gillies." The following note, upon the poem " Yarrow Visited," is of great interest. It is Wordsworth who writes.

" As mentioned in my verses on the death of the Ettrick Shepherd, my first visit to Yarrow was in his company. We had lodged the night before at Traquhar, where Hogg had joined us, and also Dr. Anderson, the editor of ' The British Poets,' who was on a visit at the manse. Dr. Anderson walked with us till we came in view of the Vale of Yarrow, and being advanced in life he then turned back. The old man was passionately fond of poetry, though with not much of a discriminating judgment, as the volumes he edited sufficiently shows; but I was much pleased to meet with him, and to acknowledge my obligation to his collection, which had been my brother John's companion in more than one voyage to India, and which he gave me before his departure from Grasmere—never to return. Through these volumes I became first familiar with Chaucer; and so little money had I then to spare for books, that in all probability, but for this same work, I should have known little of Drayton, Daniel, and other distinguished poets of the Elizabethan age, and their immediate successors, till a much later period of my life. I am glad to record this, not for any importance of its own, but as a tribute of gratitude to this simple-hearted old man, whom I never again had the pleasure of meeting. I seldom read or think of this poem without regretting that my dear sister was not of the party, as she would have been so much delighted in recalling the time when, travelling together in Scotland, we declined going in search of this celebrated stream, not altogether, I will frankly confess, for the reasons assigned in the poem on the occasion."

At last, in 1814, the great poem was published upon which Wordsworth's fame is built, viz., "The Excursion." It was met, as usual, with tremendous and most indiscriminate abuse, especially by Jeffrey, in his "This won't do" article. But despite all this, the poem grew deeply into the public mind, and is still growing there; and ranks, at last, with our highest poetry. All the characters and scenes in it are drawn from life, and there are few more interesting papers than the memoranda which the poet has left respecting these characters and their localities. "The Wanderer," he acknowledges, is chiefly an embodied idea of what he fancied *his own character might have become* in the said *Wanderer's* circumstances. His sister, with her gentle love and sweet remonstrances,—although ready to follow him to the ends of the earth—did in reality save him from this wild nomadic life, by fixing his thoughts upon a *home,* and the genial influences which domestic life would produce and exercise upon his poetic genius. And then his wife, children, and the rich harvests of fortune, which were reaped without any sowing of his, and dropped into his lap, finished the work his sister had begun, and finally settled him as a citizen and a family man. Otherwise, being strong in body, I should, he says, very probably, have " taken to the way of life such as that in which my ' Wanderer' passed the greater part of his days." Much, however, of what the " Wanderer" says and does, was the result, in verse, of the poet's experience; was what he had actually heard and seen, although refined, of course, as it passed through his imagination. He was fond of talking to all kinds of strange characters;—now treading on the outskirts of social life, or wandering with a wild, vagabond independence amongst the highways of towns and cities. Whatever of romance and adventure they had known, he wormed out of them, or *charmed* out of them; and he partially instances, as an illustration of this prying curiosity—this insatiable longing after experience, and the history of men—an old Scotchman, who married finally a relation of his wife's, and settled down at Kendal, and a travelling packman, from whom he learned much, and whose adventures and wisdom are embodied in the character of the " Wanderer." " The Solitary," "The Pastor," "Pedlar," "Margaret," "Miser," and all the dramatis personæ of the poem, are made up of veritable human materials, and had their architypes in the great world of humanity. The reader, however, must go to Dr. Wordsworth for a full relation respecting these matters. All I can add here, respecting the " Excursion," is that only 500 copies were disposed of in six years; and when, in 1827, another edition, of the same number of copies, was printed, it took seven years more to exhaust it. The poet, however, was not daunted by this culpable neglect of his immortal lines; but conscious of his own greatness, he wrote, in a letter to Southey,—" Let the age continue to love its own darkness; I shall continue to write, with, I trust, the light of heaven upon me." Jeffrey, in the pride and arrogance of his position, as Executioner General of the Courts of Critical Assize, boasted that HE—poor devil! —had *crushed* the " Excursion;" and the boast was repeated to Southey :—" Tell him," said he, Southey "that he could as soon crush Skiddaw !" Bernard Barton,—a writer whose chief merit consists in a letter written to Wordsworth, expressive of his homage and reverence for the Bard of Rydal—alludes, in the said letter, to Jeffrey: " He has taken," says Wordsworth, in reply, " a perpetual retainer, from his own incapacity, to plead against my claims to public approbation." So, we see, that the good poet could hit hard if he liked; although he rarely descended to this literary pugilism, thinking it beneath the dignity of his art and character.

It was Wordsworth's custom to compose in the open air; and as his servant once said to a visitor, " This, sir, is my master's library—his study is out of doors." He had a great and sickening dread of writing; and his sister, or some other member of his family was always at hand to perform for him the office of amanuensis. In the year 1807, when on a visit to his wife's brother at Stockton-on-Tees, the weather being very boisterous, and the winds rough, he used to pace up and down under the lee of a row of corn-stacks in a field near that town—and it was here that he composed the earlier part of " White Doe of Ryletone," chaunting his verses aloud to the astonished stacks. The poem was not published until 1815, and has been much misinterpreted, and consequently abused. The truth is, that Wordsworth wrote always upon principle, and a carefully premeditated plan; there was always a high purpose in his poems, both moral and intellectual. His poetical canons were likewise his own, and his mode of treating a subject was always in conformity with them, or illustrations of them. Superficial readers, who had been accustomed to the *objective* poetry of Scott, could not understand Wordsworth, therefore; for he was studiously *subjective*, and the interest of his poems hangs nearly always upon the development of mere spiritual forces, and their progress, if I may so speak, *outwards*, in the subjugation of the external world or in the strengthening of the soul to bear the ills and mishaps of life with a sublime fortitude. "The White Doe" is a memorable example of this spiritual aim. "Every thing," says Wordsworth, 'attempted by the principal personages in this poem *fails*, so far as its object is external and substantial; so far as it is moral and spiritual it *succeeds*. The heroine of the poem knows that her duty is not to interfere with the current of events, either to forward or delay them; but

>   "To abide
> The shock, and finally secure
> O'er pain and grief a triumph pure."

This she does in obedience to her brother's injunction, as most suitable to a mind and character that, under previous trials, had been proved to accord with his. She achieves this, not without aid from the communication with the inferior creature which often leads her thoughts to revolve upon the past with a tender and humanising influence that exalts rather than depresses her. Her anticipated beatification of the mind, and the apotheosis of the companion of her solitude, are the points at which the poem aims, and constitutes its legitimate catastrophe." All this is widely different from the usual mode of conducting dramatic action, and yet the action of the poem in question is complete and satisfactory, and is artistically developed from its own spiritual germ, or starting point.

Whilst walking, and composing "The White Doe," Wordsworth received a wound in his foot; and it is curious to remark that, even when he ceased walking, the *act of composition* increased the irritation of the wound, whilst a mental holiday produced a rapid cure. " Poetic excitement," he says, " when accompanied by protracted labour in composition, has throughout my life brought on more or less of bodily derangement. Nevertheless I am, at the close of my seventy-third year, in what may be called excellent health. But I ought to add, that my intellectual labour has generally been carried on out of doors."

The next group of poems—and two of them certainly amongst the grandest triumphs of poetic art, were composed respectively as follows :—"Laodamia," in 1814; "Dion," in 1816; and the " Ode to Lycoris," in 1817. The first and second of these poems were entirely Greek in their character and form, and Keates' " Hyperion" is the only modern poem (and this a fragment) which is worthy to be placed in comparison with them. It is singular how the idea of these poems originated in the mind of the poet. He had been preparing his son for the University, and had to read up his old classics for this purpose. Hence the Classic Spirit took up its abode with him, and urged him to these beautiful and plastic productions. About this time, and with the same object in view—viz., the education of his son—he translated one of the earlier books of the "Æneid" into rhyme. Coleridge, in writing to the author respecting this translation, says, he has attempted an impossibility, and regrets he should have wasted his time on a work (viz., of translation) so much below him. Wordsworth was always attached to the classics; and before he read Virgil, he was so fond of Ovid, that he invariably got into a passion when he found this author placed below Virgil. He was never weary of travelling over the scenes through which Homer led him. "Classical literature," he says, "affected me by its own beauty."

"Peter Bell" appeared in 1819. It was composed twenty years before, as already related; and sold better than any of Wordsworth's previous poems, notwithstanding the abuse of the critics. Five hundred copies were exhausted before one month, between April and May of this one year (1819). "The Waggoner" was published at the same time, but was not so successful, perhaps on account of its mere local interest. The "Sonnets on the River Duddon" appeared about the same time, and were dedicated to the Rev. Dr. Wordsworth, the poet's brother, who was at that time Rector of Lambeth. "The river Duddon has its main source* in the mountain range near the "Three Shire Stones," as they were called, where the three counties, Westmoreland, Cumberland, and Lancashire meet. It flows to the south through Seathwaite, by Broughton, to the Duddon Sands, and into the Irish Sea."—Wordsworth's first acquaintance with this stream commenced in his boyhood, during the time that he was so passionately fond of angling: upon one of his fishing excursions he joined an old weather-beaten man, and went far away from home, seduced by the dear delight of his art. On their return, the embryo poet was so wearied, that the old man had to carry him on his back. He says that his earliest recollections of this stream were full of distress and disappointment; but in later times he visited it with so many beloved persons, that its waters flowed through him in streams of music—in anthems of affectionate song.

In 1820 Wordsworth made another tour to the Continent, in company with his wife and

* Dr. Wordsworth's "Memoirs," vol. 2, p. 94.

sister, Mr. and Mrs. Monkhouse, then just married, and Miss Herricks. They left these two ladies at Berne, while Mr. Monkhouse went with the poet and his retinue, on an excursion amongst the Alps, as far as Milan. They were joined at Lucerne by Mr. H. C. Robinson; and the two ladies, whom they had left at Berne, rejoined them at Geneva, when the whole party went to Paris, where they remained five weeks.

In 1822 Wordsworth published a volume of Sonnets, and other Poems, as the result of this tour, entitled, "Memorials of a Tour on the Continent."

In two letters to Lord Lonsdale—one dated from Lucerne, August 19th, 1820, and the other from Paris, dated October 7, 1820,—the poet has given a general outline of this tour and its incidents.* I ought to add that Wordsworth visited Waterloo, amongst other places of interest, at this time. The party returned by way of Boulogne, November 2nd, and had a narrow escape of shipwreck,—the vessel striking upon a sand-bank, and being then

* "Memoirs," vol. 2, p. 102—105.

driven with violence on a rocky road in the harbour, where she was battered about until the ebbing of the tide set her at liberty—at least from the violence of the sea; "and, blessed be God," says Wordsworth, in his his Journal, " for our preservation !'

They arrived at Dover on the 7th, and at London on the 9th, where they met Rogers, Lamb, and Talfourd, amongst other noted persons and friends. Wordsworth walked on to visit Coleridge, from Hampstead Heath, on the 18th, and then went down to Cambridge, to congratulate his brother, Dr. Wordsworth, on his appointment to the Mastership of Trinity College.

They returned to Rydal Mount on Christmas Eve, visiting Sir George and Lady Beaumont, at Coleorton, by the way. Sir George was then about to build a church on his estate, and this fact led to conversation on Church History, and eventually to the production of the "Ecclesiastical Sonnets." In the third part of the first of these Sonnets occurs the following line:—

" I saw the figure of a lovely maid."

And the note attached to it, by the poet, is so interesting, that I must transcribe it:—

"When I came to this part of the series, I had the dream described in this sonnet. The *figure was that of my daughter*, and the whole passed exactly as here represented. The sonnet was composed on the middle road leading from Grasmere to Ambleside; it was began as I left the last house in the vale, and finished, word for word, as it now stands, before I came in view of Rydal. I wish I could say the same of the five or six hundred I have written; most of them were frequently retouched, in the course of composition, and not a few laboriously."

Here is the sonnet in question:—

" I saw the figure of a lovely maid,
Seated, alone, beneath a darksome tree,
Whose fondly-overhanging canopy
Set off her brightness with a pleasing shade.
No spirit was she; that my heart betrayed,
For she was one I loved exceedingly;
But while I gazed in tender reverie
(Or was it sleep that with my fancy played?),
The bright corporeal presence—form and face—
Remaining still distinct, grew thin and rare,
Like sunny mists; at length the golden hair,

Shape, limbs, and heavenly features, keeping pace,
Each with the other, in a lingering race
Of dissolution, melted into air."

In 1823, Wordsworth again visited the Continent, making a short tour, with his wife, in Belgium and Holland. As usual, a journal of travel was kept by the poet, and is printed, partly at least, in the "Memoirs." At the close of the summer, in the next year, he made a short excursion in North Wales, the records of which are contained in a letter to Sir George Beaumont, dated Hindwell, Radnor, September 20, 1824.* Again, in 1828, the poet, accompanied by his daughter, Dora, made an excursion to see Coleridge, through Belgium, and up the Rhine. And it was at this time that the "Incident at Bruges" was written, concerning which the poet says:—" Dora and I, while taking a walk along a retired part of the town, heard the voice as here described, and were afterwards informed that it was a Convent, in which were many English. We were both much touched, I may say, affected, and Dora moved, as appears in the verses." The "Lines

* Memoirs, vol. ii., p. 121.

on a Jewish Family," were likewise written on this tour. The poet, his daughter, and Coleridge were at St. Goar, when they first saw this family. They had provided themselves with a basket of provisions for the day, and offered the poor people a share of them. The mother refused for the rest, because it was a fast-day, adding, that whether such observances were right or wrong, it was her duty to keep them. They were all poor, ragged, and hungry, but exceedingly beautiful, and the self-command, self-respect, and self-sacrifice of the woman is the moral of this little story, I think, although no allusion is made to it in the poem.

In 1829, Wordsworth made a tour in Ireland, with J. Marshall, Esq., M.P. of Leeds. All through his life Wordsworth had a horror of Popery; and this journey, with his Continental tours, tended to confirm it with still greater intensity. He hated Popery because it was the avowed enemy of freedom, and he would not sanction the Catholic Emancipation Bill, because he thought that by giving freedom to the Catholic religion, the Government were but paving the way for a frightful domination over the souls and bodies of men. Still he loved freedom—as his sonnets to "Liberty," and his enthusiastic sympathies with republican France, at the outbreak of the first revolution sufficiently show. He was a Churchman, however, devotedly attached to the traditions, forms, and doctrines of the Church, and there was no moving him from these foundations. He attributed the distress and misery of Ireland to the priests—Catholic, of course—and to the false tenures of the land. The country, he said, had never been fully conquered, and this was another and a chief cause of the degradation of Ireland. The people were under the control —absolute control—of the priests, ready to do their bidding, let that bidding be what it might. And he trembled—as well he might—for the power of the Irish Church! God forgive us, we are all at the best but short-sighted mortals, and few can see the truth, save through the medium of prejudice. The Irish Church, if *my* vision be clear, is one of the many stumbling blocks, and rubbish heaps in the way of Irish civilization; and certainly the Roman Catholic Church is another.

This tour supplied Wordsworth with very few materials for poetry. The lines, however, in the fine poem on the "Power of Sound," one of the *finest* poems which Wordsworth has written, commencing

"Thou too be heard, lone eagle!"

were, he says, suggested near the Giant's Causeway, where he saw a pair of eagles wheel over his head, and then dart off "as if to hide themselves in a blaze of sky made by the setting sun."

It was about this time also that the sweet poem, entitled "The Triad," was written, in which the daughters of Southey, Wordsworth, and Coleridge, are bound together in the most musical and flowery forms, as the three Graces. Wordsworth often promised these fair children to send them down to immortality in his verses, but it was long before the mood seized him, and the *modus operandi* was made plain to him. At last the ideas embodied in "The Triad" struck him, and the result is something finer than the most vivid sculpture. The poet commences—

"Shew me the noblest youth of present time,
Whose trembling fancy would to love give birth;

> Some god or hero from the Olympian clime
> Returned to seek a consort upon earth;
> Or, in no doubtful prospect let me see,
> The brightest star of ages yet to be,
> And I will mate and match him blissfully."

So confident is he of the beauty and virtue of the three fair girls hidden amongst the recesses of the hills, that he boasts of their worthiness to match even the noblest of gods or heroes. And then he invokes them to appear, whilst a youth expectant at his side, and breathless as they,

> " Looks to the earth and to the vacant air;
> And with a wandering air that seems to chide,
> Asks of the clouds what occupants they hide."

And now the poet will fulfil his promise, and show the golden youth this beautiful triad of Graces.

> " Fear not a constraining measure!
> —Yielding to the gentle spell,
> Lucida! from domes of pleasure,
> Or from cottage-sprinkled dell,
> Comes to regions solitary,
> Where the eagle builds her aery,
> Above the hermit's long-forsaken cell!
> —She comes!—behold

> That figure, like a ship with silver sail!
> Nearer she draws; a breeze uplifts her veil;
> Upon her coming wait
> As pure a sunshine, and as soft a gale,
> As e'er, on herbage-covering earthly mold,
> Tempted the bird of Juno to unfold
> His richest splendour,—when his veering gait,
> And every motion of his starry train,
> Seem governed by a strain
> Of music, audible to him alone."

And then we have a picture of the lady:—

> " worthy of earth's proudest throne!
> Nor less, by excellence of nature, fit
> Beside an unambitious hearth to sit
> Domestic queen, where grandeur is unknown;
> What living man could fear
> The worst of fortune's malice, wer't thou near,
> Humbling that lily stem, thy sceptre meek,
> That its fair flowers may brush from off his cheek
> The too, too, happy tear?
> —Queen, and handmaid lowly!
> Whose skill can speed the day with lively cares,
> And banish melancholy
> By all that mind invents, or hand prepares;
> O thou, against whose lip, without its smile
> And in its silence even, no heart is proof;
> Whose goodness, sinking deep, would reconcile
> The softest nursling of a gorgeous palace,
> To the bare life beneath the hawthorn roof

Of Sherwood's archer, or in caves of Wallace—
Who that hath seen thy beauty could content
His soul with but a *glimpse* of heavenly day?
Who that hath loved thee, but would lay
His strong hand on the wind, if it were bent
To take thee in thy majesty away?
Pass onward (even the glancing deer
Till we depart intrude not here;)
That mossy slope, o'er which the woodbine throws
A canopy, is smooth'd for thy repose!"

The next lady that he invokes before the astonished youth is his own daughter—sweet Dora—the previous one was Miss Southey.

" Come, if the notes thine ear may pierce,
Come, youngest of the lovely three,
Submissive to the mighty verse
And the dear voice of harmony,
By none more deeply felt than thee!
I sang; and lo! from pastures virginal
She hastens to the haunts
Of Nature, and the lonely elements.
Air sparkles round her with a dazzling sheen;
And mark, her glowing cheek, her vesture green!
And, as if wishful to disarm
Or to repay the potent charm,
She bears the stringed lute of old romance,
That cheered the trellissed arbour's privacy,
And soothed war-wearied knights in raftered hall.

How vivid, yet how delicate, her glee!
So tripped the muse, inventress of the dance;
So, truant in waste woods, the blithe Euphrosyne!"

But the ringlets of that head,
Why are they ungarlanded?
Why bedeck her temples less
Than the simplest shepherdess?
Is it not a brow inviting
Choicest flowers that ever breathed,
Which the myrtle would delight in,
With Idalian rose enwreathed?
But her humility is well content
With *one* wild floweret (call it not forlorn),—
Flower of the Winds—beneath her bosom worn—
Yet more for love than ornament."

Then follows that beautiful description of her moral graces, already quoted in these pages, beginning—

" Open ye thickets! let her fly,
Swift as a Thracian nymph, o'er field and height;"

the whole picture being as fine a conception, and as rich an embodyment, of this sweet Dora, —judging from her portrait in the second volume of the " Memoirs," and from numerous written and spoken reports of her person and character,—as the highest genius and the highest art combined, could possibly have produced. And now for Miss Coleridge :—

" Last of the three, tho' eldest born,
Reveal thyself, like pensive morn
Touched by the skylark's earliest note,
E'er humble-gladness be afloat.
But whether in the semblance drest
Of dawn, or eve, fair vision of the west,
Come, with each anxious hope subdued
By woman's gentle fortitude,
Each grief, thro' meekness, settling into rest.
—Or I would hail thee when some high-wrought page
Of a closed volume, lingering in thine hand,
Has raised thy spirit to a peaceful stand
Among the glories of a happy age."

And, behold! she is here :—

" Her brow hath opened on me—see it there,
Brightening the umbrage of her hair;
So gleams the crescent moon, that loves
To be descried thro' shady groves.
Tenderest bloom is on her cheek;
Wish not for a richer streak;
Nor *dread the depth of meditative eye;*
But let thy love, upon that azure field
Of thoughtfulness and beauty, yield
Its homage offered up in purity.
What would'st thou more? In sunny glade,
Or under leaves of thickest shade,

Was such a stillness e'er diffused
Since earth grew calm while angels mused?
Softly she treads, as if her foot were loth
To crush the mountain dew-drop—soon to melt,
On the flower's breast; as if she felt
That flowers themselves, whate'er their hue,
With all their fragrance, all their glistening,
Call to the heart for inward listening—
And tho' for bridal wreaths and tokens true
Welcomed wisely; tho' a growth
Which the careless shepherd sleeps on,
As fitly spring from turf the mourner weeps on—
And without wrong are cropped the marble tomb to strew.

And now the charm is over;

———" the mute phantom's gone,
Nor will return—but droop not, favoured youth,
The apparition that before thee shone
Obeyed a summons covetous of truth.
From these wild rocks thy footsteps I will guide
To bowers in which thy fortunes may be tried,
And one of the bright three become thy happy bride."

A fairer subject than this, for the imagination of the true painter, does scarcely exist in poetry. The gorgeous magnificence of Miss Southey—the wild, bird-like nature of Dora, the mystic, spiritual, meditative beauty of Miss Coleridge.

Here is material enough for the highest effort of art.

A number of poems followed this exquisite "Triad"—viz., "The Wishing Gate," in 1828— "The Lawn," "Presentiments," "The Primrose on the Rock," "Devotional Incitements;" these last were written between 1828 and '32. A number of gold and silver fishes presented to the poet by Miss H. J. Jewsbury, who subsequently died of the cholera in India,—and afterwards removed to the pond already alluded to, under the oak in "Dora's field," suggested the verses "Gold and Silver Fishes in a Vase," and likewise "Liberty," and "Humanity;" "The Poet and the caged Turtle Dove" was likewise suggested by real circumstances. Miss Jewsbury had given Dora a pair of these beautiful birds; one of them was killed by an *un*-necessary cat, and not a "harmless one;" the other survived many years, and had a habit of cooing the moment Wordsworth began "booing" his poems, as the country people called it.

Wordsworth gives an amusing account of a visit which he paid about this time to "Chatsworth." He had undertaken to ride his daughter's pony from Westmoreland to Cambridge, that she might have the use of it during a visit she was about to make to her uncle at Trinity; and on his way from Bakewell to Matlock, he turned off to see the splendid mansion of the great Duke of Devonshire. By-and-bye a tremendous storm came on, and the poet was drenched through to the very skin, whilst the pony, to make his rider's seat the more easy, went "slantwise" all the way to Derby. Notwithstanding this, however, and the pelting of the pitiless storm, Wordsworth managed to hold sweet and sad converse with his muse, and composed his "Lines to the Memory of Sir George Beaumont," who died 7th February, 1827. It is a picture which we cannot readily forget, and shows how completely the poet was master of himself. Sir George Beaumont and his lady were friends and benefactors of Wordsworth—he loved them both intensely. Walking through the grounds and gardens of Coleorton with Sir George— the successor in the Baronetcy to his friend— and after the death of Lady Beaumont, which took place in 1822, he comes suddenly to her ladyship's grotto, near the fountain, and is overwhelmed with his feelings, and the recollection of the dead, and the happy memories which rush over his mind in connection with this place, so that he cannot speak for tears. On his return home he wrote the elegiac musings, already mentioned in these memoirs, which are full of love, and the sanctity of a sweet sorrow. In the same year (1831) were composed " The Armenian Lady's Love," " The Egyptian Maid," and " The Russian Fugitive," poems in which all the beauties of language are pressed, along with the simplicity which marks the old English ballads. Lines on his portrait, painted by Pickersgill, and preserved with sacred veneration in St. John's College, Cambridge, were likewise written in this year, as well as the inscription already quoted, for the stone at Rydal.

Besides these poetical compositions, however, Wordsworth interested himself in public affairs; and having fixed principles of political and social economy in his own mind, regarded all public measures at variance with them, as fatal errors, and subversive in their consequences of the highest human concerns. In 1806, he wrote a letter to a friend, who had consulted him respecting the education of his daughter—in which he gives some sound and excellent advice respecting the training and development of youthful minds. For Wordsworth had at an early period devoted his attention to the subject of education, and had his own views respecting it—views which were marked by the spiritual peculiarity of his mind. When he wrote "The Excursion," he seems to have had the highest hopes for man, when education should become universal; and insisted that the State should teach those to obey, from whom she exacted allegiance :—

> " O for the coming of that glorious time,
> When, prizing knowledge, as her noblest work
> And best protection, this imperial realm
> While she exacts allegiance, shall admit
> An obligation on her part to *teach*
> Them who are born to serve her and obey;
> Binding herself, by statute, to secure
> For all the children whom her soil maintains
> The rudiments of letters, and inform
> The mind with moral and religious truth,
> Both understood, and practised."
> *Excursion*, Book ix.

He was an avowed enemy, however, at a later period—for his views respecting the *modus operandi* of teaching, had undergone some change since " The Excursion" was written— to all Infant Schools, Madras Systems, and Bell Systems. The former he regarded as usurping the functions of motherly duty; the latter, as dead mechanism. Speaking of the education of girls, he says:—" I will back Shenstone's 'School Mistress,' by her winter fire, and in her summer garden seat, against all Dr. Bell's sour-looking teachers in petticoats. What is the use of pushing on the education of girls so fast, and moving by the stimulus of Emulation, who, to say nothing worse of her, is cousin-german to Envy? What are you to do with these girls? What demand is there for the ability that they may have prematurely acquired? Will they not be indisposed to bend to any kind of hard labour or drudgery? And yet many of them must submit to it, or go wrong. The mechanism of the Bell System is not required in small places; praying after the *fugleman,* is not like praying at a mother's knee. The Bellites overlook the difference: they talk about moral discipline; but wherein does it encourage the imaginative feelings? in short, what she practically understands is of little amount, and too apt to become the slave of the bad passions. I dislike *display* in everything; above all, in education. . . . The old dame (Shenstone's) did not affect to make theologians and logicians; but she taught to read; and she practised the memory, often no doubt by rote, but still the faculty was improved; something, perhaps, she explained, but trusted the *rest* to parents and masters, and to the pastor of the parish. I am sure as good daughters, as good servants, as good mothers and wives, were brought up at that time as now, when the world is so much less humble-minded. A hand full of employment, and a head not above it, with such principles and habits as may be acquired *without* the Madras machine, are the best security for the chastity of wives of the lower rank."

The above extract is from a letter dated 1828, and addressed to the Rev. Hugh Jones Rose, formerly principal of King's College, London. It exemplifies, in a very striking manner, the change which had come over Wordsworth's mind upon the subject of education, and does not strike me as being particularly creditable to him.

On the 13th of April, 1836, Wordsworth took part in the ceremony of laying the foundation-stone of certain new schools, about to be erected at Bowness, Windermere, and made a speech upon the occasion; in which he advocates a very humble kind of instruction for the working classes; forgetting that man is to be educated because he *is a man*, and not neglected because he happens to be one of the "lower orders." I have no sympathy with this foolish cant about educating people according to their station, and am sorry that Wordsworth's sanction can be quoted in its favour. I must reserve what I have to say upon this subject, however, for my analysis of the mind and writings of the poet.

In 1835, Wordsworth published his "Yarrow Revisited, and other Poems." Speaking of "Yarrow Re-visited," he says: "In the autumn of 1831, my daughter and I set off from Rydal, to visit Sir Walter Scott, before his departure for Italy. This journey had been delayed by an inflammation in my eyes, till we found that the time appointed for his leaving home would be too near for him to receive us without considerable inconvenience. Nevertheless we proceeded, and reached Abbotsford on Monday. I was then scarcely able to lift up my eyes to the light. How sadly changed did I find him from the man I had seen so healthy, gay, and hopeful, a few years before, when he said, at the inn at Patterdale, in my presence, his daughter, Ann, also being there, with Mr. Lockhart, my own wife and daughter, and Mr. Quillinan: 'I mean to live till I am eighty, and shall write as long as I live.' Though we had none of us the least thought of the cloud of misfortune which was then going to break upon his head, I was startled, and almost shocked, at that bold saying, which could scarcely be uttered by such a man, without a momentary forgetfulness of the instability of human life. But to return to Abbotsford. The inmates and guests we found there, were Sir Walter, Major Scott, Anne Scott, and Mr. and Mrs. Lockhart; Mr. Laidlaw, a very old friend of Sir Walter's; one of Burns's sons, an officer of the Indian service, had left the house the day before, and had kindly expressed his regret that he could not wait my arrival, a regret that I may truly say was mutual. In the evening, Mr. and Mrs. Liddell sang, and Mrs. Lockhart chaunted old ballads to her harp; and Mr. Allan, hanging over the back of a chair, told, and acted, odd stories in a humourous way. With this exhibition, and his daughters' singing, Sir Walter was much amused, and, indeed, so were we all, as far as circumstances would allow."

On the following morning (Tuesday) Sir Walter accompanied Wordsworth, and most of his friends, to Newark Castle, on the Yarrow, and it was upon this occasion that the lines, "Yarrow Revisited," were written. On the morning of Thursday following, when the poet left Abbotsford, he had a serious conversation with Sir Walter, who spoke with gratitude of the happy life he had led. Sir Walter wrote also a few lines in Dora's album, addressed to her; and when he presented her with the book, in his study, he said: "I should not have done a thing of this kind, but for your father's sake; they are probably the last verses I shall ever write." "They shew," says, Wordsworth, "how much his mind was impaired; not by the strain of thought, but by the execution—some of the lines being imperfect, and one stanza wanting corresponding rhymes." Poor Sir Walter!—

what a spectacle it was to see that colossal intellect tumbling into ruins.

Several poems were the result of this short tour, beside the "Yarrow Revisited,"—such as "The Place of Burial," "On the Sight of a Manse in the South of Scotland," &c., &c.— Wordsworth's health, too, was much improved by this tour, and a violent inflammation of the eyes—a complaint to which he was much subject,—left him whilst walking through the Highlands, by the side of his "open carriage," driven by Dora!

Amongst the poems contained in the volume entitled, "Yarrow Revisited," were many of a political character, for they were written between the years 1830 and 1834, when the Revolution of France, and the Reform party in England, were agitating society to its centre. Wordsworth now hated revolution, and reform also; was opposed to a large and enlightened system of education; and to the admission of Dissenters to the Universities. His plea was the old constitution of things, which could not, he thought, be mended without being broken up and destroyed. "Since the introduction of the Reform Bill, I have been persuaded," he says, "that the Constitution of England cannot be preserved. It is a question, however, of time." The poem entitled, "The Warning," will give the best idea of Wordsworth's strong political opinions and feelings at this time. As a contrast, however, to these narrow yet patriotic views, we turn to the "Evening Voluntaries," a collection of sweet poems, which were published in the same volume as the "Yarrow." They were written on a high part of the coast of Cumberland, on April 7th (Easter Sunday), the author's 63rd birth-day, between Moresby and Whitehaven, whilst he was on a visit to his son, who was then rector of Moresby.— Very beautiful, indeed, are these poems, which read like twilight vespers in some old abbey's chancel. Wordsworth says of them—" With the exception of the eighth and ninth, this succession of voluntaries originated in the concluding lines of the last paragraph of this poem, [i.e. of the poem, written on the author's birth-day, and marked No. 2, in the "Voluntaries," commencing, "The sun that seemed so mildly to retire."] With this coast I have been familiar from my earliest childhood, and remember being struck, for the first time, by the town and port of Whitehaven, and the white waves breaking against its quays and piers, as the whole came into my view from the top of the high ground, down which the road, that has since been altered, descended abruptly. My sister, when she first heard the voice of the sea from this point, and beheld the scene spread before her, burst into tears. Our family then lived at Cockermouth, and this fact was often mentioned amongst us, indicating the sensibility for which she was remarkable."

As a specimen of the "Evening Voluntaries," take the following :—

"Calm is the air, and loth to lose
Day's grateful warmth, tho' moist with falling dews.
Look for the stars, you'll say that there are none;
Look up a second time, and one by one,
You mark them twinkling out with silvery light,
And wonder how they could elude the sight!
The birds, of late so noisy in their bowers,
Warbled awhile with faint and fainter powers,
But now are silent as the dim-seen flowers.
Nor does the village church clock's iron tone
The time's and season's influence disown;
Nine beats distinctly to each other bound
In drowsy sequence—how unlike the sound
That in rough winter, oft inflicts a fear
On fireside listeners, doubting what they hear!

The shepherd, bent on rising with the sun,
Had closed his door before the day was done,
And now with thankful heart to bed doth creep,
And joins the little children in their sleep.
The bat, lured forth where trees the lane o'ershade,
Flits and reflits along the dark arcade;
The busy dor-hawk chases the white moth
With burring note, which industry and sloth
Might both be pleased with, for it suits them both.
A stream is heard—I see it not but know
By its soft music where the waters flow:
Wheels and the tread of hoofs are heard no more;
One boat there was, but it will touch the shore
With the next dipping of its slackened oar;
Faint sound that for the gayest of the gay,
Might give to serious thought a moment's sway,
As a last token of man's toilsome day."

Wordsworth does not seem, during any period of his life, to have been on intimate terms with any of his contemporaries. He preferred the flower of the literateurs, Coleridge, Scott, Southey; and these, with the exception perhaps of Rogers, were his chief friends. We have letters of his, however, to much smaller fry; to Mrs. Hemans, and Miss Jewsbury, for example—and to sundry editors of other men's wares; but there is little or no recognition of Byron, Shelly, Keats, Tennyson, Baily, Campbell, Moore, nor yet of Dickens or Bulwer. His letters represent his character even better than his poetry; they are Wordsworth in undress, without the "garland and singing robe," and are worthy to be studied. I like much what he says to the Rev. Robert Montgomery, author of "The Devil and Father Luther," and pious Robert would do well even at this late day to think on it. Montgomery had sent Wordsworth a copy of his poems, and in reply, the poet answers: "I cannot conclude without one word of literary advice which I hope you will deem my advanced age entitles me to give. Do not, my dear sir, be anxious about any individual's opinion concerning your writings, however highly you may think of his genius, or rate his judgment. Be a severe critic to yourself; and depend upon it no person's decision upon the merit of your works will bear comparison in point of value with your own. You must be conscious from what feeling they have flowed, and how far they may or may not be allowed to claim on that account, permanent respect; and above all I would remind you, with a view to tranquillise and steady your mind, that no man takes the trouble of surveying and pondering another's writings with a hundredth part of the care which an author of sense and genius will have bestowed upon his own. Add to this reflection another, which I press upon you, as it has supported me through life—viz.: That posterity will settle all accounts justly, and that works which deserve to last will last; and if undeserving this fate, the sooner they perish the better."

In the year 1836 the sister of the poet's wife—Miss Sarah Hutchinson, who had resided with the family at Rydal, died, and was buried in Grasmere church, " near the graves of two young children removed from a family to which through life she was devoted."

In the following year, 1837, Wordsworth, accompanied by his friend H. C. Robinson, Esq., set off from London for Rome, returning in August. The " Itinerary" of the travellers is contained in the " Memoirs," along with some memoranda by the poet; but they are not of much interest. Many fine pieces, however, sprung as usual from the journey, as well as a goodly number of sonnets. They originally appeared in a volume entitled " Poems, chiefly of Early and Late Years," in 1842. In 1839, Wordsworth received the degree of D.C.L., from the University of Oxford, which was conferred on him in the Sheldonian Theatre, amidst shouts of rejoicing such as had never before been heard in that city, except upon the occasion of an unexpected visit of the Duke of Wellington. In 1838, Wordsworth prepared a new edition of his poems, to be published by Moxon, and continued to live at Rydal, in his quiet and musical manner, writing poems, taking rambles, and conducting his correspondence until 1843, when he was appointed Poet Laureate of England, Southey having died on the 21st of March of that year, and the appointment having been offered to Wordsworth on the 31st of the same month. One occurrence only broke the even tenor of the poet's life in the interim alluded to, and this was an accident by which he was upset from his gig, and thrown violently into a plantation. The accident was owing to the carelessness and want of skill in the driver of a coach, which they met on the road. No serious consequences followed, however, and inquiries and congratulations flowed in on all sides, from the peasant up to Queen Adelaide.

From the time of Wordsworth's appointment as Laureate,—which it ought to be said he at first refused, and only accepted with the understanding that it should be an honorary office,—he wrote very little poetry. His work, indeed, was done, his mission accomplished; and his old days were spent in rambling over the hills, and in the quiet enjoyment of his family, friends, fame, and fortune. Honours of a high order were subsequently heaped upon him. In the year 1838, the University of Durham took the initiative in conferring an academic degree on the poet; then the grand old Mother, Oxford, followed,—and in 1846 he was put in nomination, without his knowledge, for the office of Lord Rector of the University of Oxford, and gained a majority of twenty-one votes, in opposition to the premier, Lord John Russell. "The forms of election, however," says Wordsworth, in a letter to Sir W. Gomm, of Port Louis, Mauritius, dated November 23, 1846, "allowed Lord John Russell to be returned through the single vote of the sub-rector voting for his superior. To say the truth, I am glad of this result, being too advanced in life to undertake with comfort any considerable public duty, and it might have seemed ungracious to have declined the office."

On the 20th of January, 1847, Mr. William Wordsworth, the younger son of the poet, was married at Brighton, to Fanny Eliza Graham, youngest daughter of Reginald Graham, Esq., of Brighton, who was a native of Cumberland; and whilst the joy of this event was still fresh in the hearts of the Rydal household, a dread calamity awaited them in the death of Mrs. Quillinan—the sweet Dora so often spoken of in these pages, the beloved daughter of the poet. As previously stated, she had accompanied her husband to Portugal for the benefit of her health,—and although the change seemed at first to have operated favourably upon her, it was soon evident, on her return home, that she was doomed for the silent bourne of all travellers in this world. She died on the 9th day of July, 1847, and was buried in Grasmere church-yard. Her death was a terrible blow to the venerable poet, now in his eightieth year,—but he bore up patiently, with the heart and hope of a Christian.

Three years after this sad loss, Wordsworth himself was summoned away. On Sunday, the

10th of March, 1850, he attended at Rydal chapel for the last time, visiting, during the day, a poor old woman, who had once been his servant, and another person who was sick, and as the poet said, " never complained."

"On the afternoon of the following day, he went towards Grasmere, to meet his two nieces, who were coming from Town End. He called at the cottage near the White Moss Quarry, and the occupant being within, *he sat down on the stone seat of the porch, to watch the setting sun.* It was a cold, bright day. His friend and neighbour, Mr. Roughsedge, came to drink tea at Rydal, but Mr. Wordsworth not being well, went early to bed."

From this time he gradually grew worse; and in order to convey to him the impressions of his physicians, Mrs. Wordsworth whispered in a soft voice, full of deep devotion, " Dear William, you are going to Dora." How delicate, how affectionate, how poetical! But the poet did not hear, or did not seem to hear; and yet, twenty-four hours after, when one of his nieces came into the room, and gently drew aside the curtains of his bed, he caught a glimpse of her figure, and asked, "Is that Dora?"

On the 23rd of April—the birth-day, and death-day of Shakspeare, the great-hearted Wordsworth went back again to God.

He was buried on the 27th, in Grasmere church-yard.

Those who would know more of the poet must go to his writings; and, I may add, that the "Memoirs" of Dr. Wordsworth are indispensable to a full understanding both of the Poet and the Man. His letters, containing his most private thoughts, are printed there with plentiful profuseness; and the "Memoranda" respecting the origin of his poems are intensely interesting and important to all students of Wordsworth. The reminiscences of various persons who knew him, set the character of the poet before us in strong relief. All agree in speaking of him as a most kindly, affectionate, and hospitable man, living with the simple tastes and manners of a patriarch, in his beautiful home. My limits prevent me from entering into an analysis of his mind and character, as I had intended to do; I must reserve this work, therefore, for another occasion, and will conclude with a few quotations from the poet's

"Table-Talk," respecting his cotemporaries.—Speaking of Goethe, he says:—

"He does not seem to me to be a great poet in either of the classes of poets. At the head of the first I would place Homer and Shakspeare, whose universal minds are able to reach every variety of thought and feeling, without bringing his own individuality before the reader. They infuse, they breathe life into every object they approach, but you cannot find *themselves.* At the head of the second class, those whom you can trace individually in all they write, I would place Spenser and Milton. In all that Spenser writes, you can trace the gentle, affectionate spirit of the man; in all that Milton writes, you find the exalted, sustained being that he was. Now, in what Goethe writes, who aims to be of the first class, the *universal,* you find the man himself, the artificial man, where he should not be found; so that I consider him a very artificial writer, aiming to be universal, and yet constantly exposing his individuality, which his character was not of a kind to dignify. He had not sufficiently clear moral perceptions to make him anything but an artificial writer.

And again :—

"I have tried to read Goethe. I never could succeed. Mr. —— refers me to his 'Iphigenia,' but I there recognise none of the dignified simplicity, none of the health and vigour which the heroes and heroines of antiquity possess in the writings of Homer. The lines of Lucretius describing the immolation of Iphigenia are worth the whole of Goethe's long poem. Again there is a profligacy, an inhuman sensuality, in his works, which is utterly revolting. I am not intimately acquainted with them generally. But I take up my ground on the first canto of 'Wilhelm Meister;' and as the attorney-general of human nature, I there indict him for wantonly outraging the sympathies of humanity. Theologians tell us of the degraded nature of man; and they tell us what is true. Yet man is essentially a moral agent, and there is that immortal and unextinguishable yearning for something pure and spiritual which will plead against these poetical sensualists as long as man remains what he is."

Of Scott he says :—

"As a poet, Scott cannot live, for he has never in verse written anything addressed to the immortal part of man. In making amusing stories in verse, he will be superseded by some newer versifier; what he writes in the way of natural description is merely rhyming nonsense. As a prose writer, Mr. Wordsworth admitted that Scott had touched a higher vein, because there he had really dealt with feeling and passion. As historical novels, professing to give the manners of a past time, he did not attach much value to those works of Scott's, so called, because that he held to be an attempt in which success was impossibility. This led to some remarks on historical writing, from which it appeared that Mr. Wordsworth has small value for anything but contemporary history. He laments that Dr. Arnold should have spent so much of his time and powers in gathering up, and putting into imaginary shape, the scattered fragments of the history of Rome."

And again :—

" He discoursed at great length on Scott's works. His poetry he considered of that kind which will always be in demand, and that the supply will always meet it, suited to the age. He does not consider that it in any way goes below the surface of things; it does not reach to any intellectual or spiritual emotion; it is altogether superficial, and he felt it himself to be so. His descriptions are not true to nature; they are addressed to the ear, not to the mind. He was a master of bodily movements in his battle-scenes; but very little productive power was exerted in popular creations."

Moore :—

" T. Moore has great natural genius; but he is too lavish of brilliant ornament. His poems smell of the perfumer's and milliner's shops. He is not content with a ring and a bracelet, but he must have rings in the ear, rings on the nose—rings everywhere."

Shelley :—

" Shelley is one of the best *artists* of us all: I mean in workmanship of style."

Tennyson :—

" I saw Tennyson, when I was in London, several times. He is decidedly the first of our living poets, and I hope will live to give the world still better things. You will be pleased to hear that he expressed in the strongest terms his gratitude to my writings. To this I was far from indifferent, though persuaded that he is not much in sympathy with what I should myself most value in my attempts—viz., the spirituality with which I have endeavoured to invest the material universe, and the moral relations under which I have wished to exhibit its most ordinary appearances."

Hartley Coleridge—

He spoke of with affection. "There is a single line," he added, " in one of his father's poems, which I consider explains the after life of the son. He is speaking of his own confinement in London, and then says,—

' But thou, my child, shalt wander like a breeze.'

" He thought highly also of some of Hartley's sonnets.

Southey—

He said had outlived his faculties. His mind he thought had been wrecked by long watching by the sick bed of his wife, who had lingered for years in a very distressing state.

Coleridge—

He said the liveliest and truest image he could give of Coleridge's talk was that of " a mystic river, the sound or sight of whose course you caught at intervals, which was sometimes concealed by forests, sometimes lost in sand, and then came flashing out broad and distinct; then again took a turn which your eye could not follow, yet you knew and felt that it was the same river.* .... Coleridge had been

---

*This view of Coleridge is confirmed by Carlyle, in his "Life of John Sterling," just published.

" Coleridge sat on the brow of Highgate-hill, in those years, looking down on London and its smoke-tumult, like a sage escaped from the inanity of life's battle; attracting towards him the thoughts of innumerable brave souls still engaged there. His express contributions to poetry, philosophy, or any specific province of human literature or enlightenment, had been small and sadly intermittent; but he had, especially among young inquiring men, a higher than literary,—a kind of prophetic, or magician character. He was thought to hold,—he alone in England,—the key of German and other transcendentalisms; knew the sublime secret of believing by 'the reason' what 'the understanding' had been obliged to fling out as incredible; and could still, after Hume and Voltaire had done their best and worst with him, profess himself an orthodox Christian, and say and point to the Church of England, with its singular old rubrics and surplices at Allhallowtide, *Esto perpetua.* * * * * He distinguished himself to all that ever heard him as at least the most *surprising* talker extant in this world,—and to some small minority, (by no

spoilt as a poet by going to Germany. The bent of his mind, at all times very much inclined to metaphysical theology, had there been fixed in that direction."

Lord Byron—

" Has spoken severely of my compositions.

means to all,) the most excellent. The good man, he was now getting old, towards sixty perhaps,—and gave you the idea of a life that had been full of sufferings; a life heavy-laden, half-vanquished, still swimming painfully in seas of manifold physical and other bewilderment. * *
 * * * I still recollect his 'object' and 'subject,' terms of continual recurrence in the Kantean province; and how he sung and snuffled them into 'omm-mject' 'sum-m-mject,' with a kind of solemn shake or quaver, as he rolled along. No talk, in his century or in any other, could be more surprising.
 * * * * *
" He had knowledge about many things and topics,— much curious reading; but generally all topics led him, after a pass or two, into the high seas of theosophic philosophy, the hazy infinitude of Kantean transcendentalism, with its 'sum-m-mjects' and 'om m-mjects.' Sad enough, for with such indolent impatience of the claims and ignorances of others, he had not the least talent for explaining this or anything unknown to them; and you swam and fluttered in the mistiest, wide, unintelligible deluge of things,—for most part in a rather profitless, uncomfortable manner. Glorious islets, too, I have seen rise out of the

However faulty they may be, I do not think I ever could have prevailed with myself to print such lines as he has done, for instance—

> 'I stood at Venice on the Bridge of Sighs,
> A palace and a prison on each hand.'

"Some person ought to write a critical review analising Lord Byron's language, in order to guard others against imitating him in these respects."

Emerson and Carlyle—

"Do you know Miss Peabody of Boston? She has just sent me, with the highest eulogy, certain essays of Mr. Emerson. Our —— and haze; but they were few, and soon swallowed in the general element again. * * * *
* * One right peal of concrete laughter at some convicted flesh-and-blood absurdity, one burst of noble indignation at some injustice or depravity rubbing elbows with us on this solid earth,—how strange would it have been in that Kantean haze-world, and how infinitely cheering amid its vacant air-castles, and dim-melting ghosts and shadows! None such ever came. His life had been an abstract thinking and dreaming, idealistic one, passed amid the ghosts of defunct bodies and of unborn ones. The mourning sing-song of that theosophico-metaphysical monotony left on you, at last, a very dreary feeling."

he appear to be what the French called *esprits forts*, though the French idols showed their spirit after a somewhat different fashion. Our two present *Philosophes*, who have taken a language which they suppose to be English, for their vehicle, are, verily, *par nobile fratrum*, and it is a pity that the weakness of our age has not left them exclusively to this appropriate reward—mutual admiration. Where is the thing which now passes for philosophy at Boston to stop?"

Such are a few random selections from the spoken opinions of the poet. He hated innovation, hence his attack upon the two last named authors, not made, I think, in the very best spirit. I must here leave him, however. He will stand well upon his honours in all future generations, and must certainly be ranked as a poet in the same category with Milton.

FINIS.

J. S. Pratt, Stokesley, Yorkshire.

UNIVERSITY OF CALIFORNIA LIBRARY
BERKELEY

Return to desk from which borrowed.
This book is DUE on the last date stamped below.

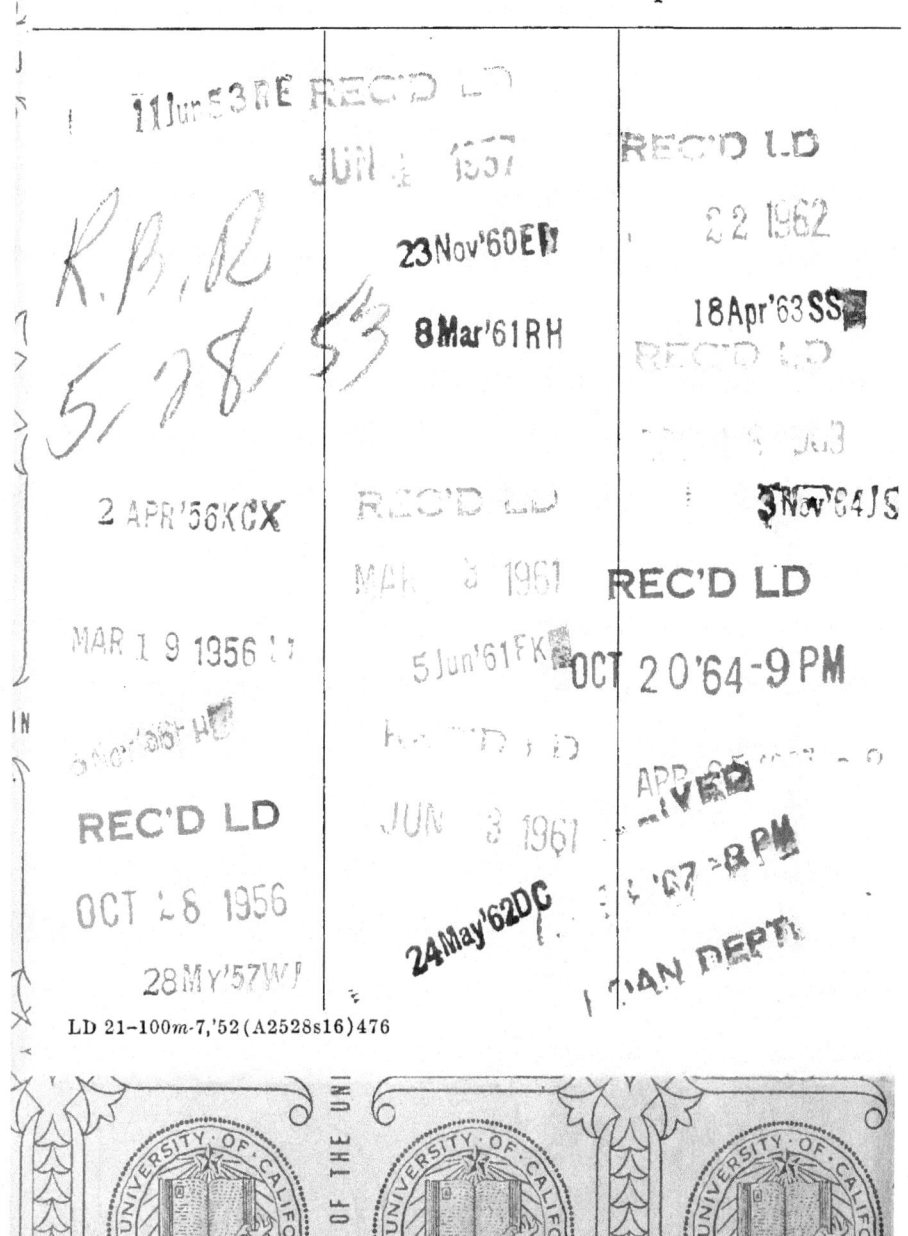

ImTheStory.com

Personalized Classic Books in many genre's

Unique gift for kids, partners, friends, colleagues

Customize:
- Character Names
- Upload your own front/back cover images (optional)
- Inscribe a personal message/dedication on the inside page (optional)

Customize many titles Including
- Alice in Wonderland
- Romeo and Juliet
- The Wizard of Oz
- A Christmas Carol
- Dracula
- Dr. Jekyll & Mr. Hyde
- And more...

Emily's Adventures in Wonderland

Ryan & Julia